Milan and the Italian Lakes

- A ☛ in the text denotes a highly recommended sight
- A complete A–Z of practical information starts on p.102
- Extensive mapping on cover flaps and throughout text

Berlitz Publishing Company, Inc.
Princeton Mexico City Dublin Eschborn Singapore

Original Text: Jack Altman
Photography: John Davison, Action-Plus and LAT Photographic
Editor: Bowman Hastie
Layout: Media Content Marketing, Inc.
Cartography: GeoSystems Global Corporation

Although we make every effort to ensure the accuracy of all information in this book, changes do occur. If you find an error in this guide, please let our editors know by writing to us at Berlitz Publishing Company, 400 Alexander Park, Princeton, NJ 08540-6306. A postcard will do.

ISBN 2-8315-6978-8

Revised 1998 — First Printing September 1998

Printed in Italy
019/809 REV

CONTENTS

Milan

MILAN AND THE MILANESE

If Rome is the heart of Italy, Milan is its head. This is a city that vigorously rejects the narrow parochialism which besets so many other Italian centres, not excluding Rome itself. Located in the Po Valley on the country's northern "outskirts," Milan faces across the Alps the mighty cultural and commercial powers of Germany and France. As capital of Lombardy, it shares the valley with the university town of Pavia; hilltop Bergamo, stylish outpost of the Venetian empire; and, on the way east to Lake Garda, the lively industrial city of Brescia.

To the west and east are the tributaries of the Po—the Ticino, flowing out of Lake Maggiore, and the Adda, coming down from Lake Como, respectively—while to the south is the fertile valley plain with its crops of wheat, maize, sugar-beet, and, in marshy corners, paddy fields of rice.

Just 50 km (30 miles) to the north lies the Swiss border, cutting through the amphitheatre formed by the foothills of the Alps.

By rights, for its energy, style and economic power, Milan should be the capital of Italy. To get a feel for Italian creativity today, for better and for worse, this is the place to be. In industry, fashion, and commerce, the city sets both tastes and standards for the whole country and much of Europe, too. While Rome and much of the rest of Italy sometimes seem to be resting with narcissistic charm on the laurels of a long history, Milan has an image that is elegant but also industrious, vibrant, and outward- and forward-looking.

Yet Milan can in no way challenge Rome's first claim on the popular imagination. Other than a few Corinthian columns at the old Porta Ticinese town gate, it lacks any substantial links with the ancient classical world. What's more, despite the presence of Leonardo da Vinci and the splendid art collection of the Brera and other museums, the city remained peripheral to the major achievements of the Renaissance era.

Symbolically, however, with the passing of the great age of Italian cinema epitomized in Rome by Federico Fellini, Milan has become the production centre for the aggressive new age of television. Far from being a purely 20th-century phenomenon, this provocative modernity has always characterized the city. In constructing its cathedral, Milan was not content with building Italy's largest Gothic monument; over the centuries, it added literally scores of spires in a bold statement of the city's flamboyant spirit.

When seeking employment with Ludovico, Duke of Milan, Leonardo da Vinci boasted of his talents as a civil and military engineer, offered to design a monument to the duke's late

The view of Milan from the roof of the Duomo is a juxtaposition of the new and the old.

father, and mentioned only incidentally that he was quite a good painter, too. Today, you can enjoy not only Leonardo's sublime, newly restored *Last Supper,* but also a grand museum of his revolutionary machines, aircraft and all.

Painting of all styles still flourishes in the heart of Milan.

Although Napoleon conquered many great cities around Europe, only Milan thought of erecting a statue of him in the nude, right in front of the Brera Museum. Among 19th-century edifices, the Galleria Vittorio Emanuele is not just another shopping arcade, but an eloquent tribute to the industrial age of steel and glass. Then there is La Scala opera house: unprepossessing as it may look from the outside, in its interior and sublime prestige it stands as a monument of quasi-sacred dimensions throughout the world.

Moving forward, the city's 1920s railway station, the absurdly pompous Stazione Centrale, is an apt expression of Mussolini's ugly version of the modern age. The graceful Pirelli skyscraper directly opposite makes an aesthetically welcome response.

If all this modernity gets to be too much, you can always wander away from it with a stroll along the 16th-century Navigli canals by the Porta Ticinese gate or in the gardens behind the Castello Sforzesco.

Milanese are frenetic football tifosi (supporters), whether in the Meazza Stadium or the giardini publici.

Living in Style

Milan's strategic location as a gateway between northern Europe and Italy attracted many invaders, notably the Spanish, French, and Austrians. It was the Austrians of the 19th-century Habsburg empire, however, who left the most visible mark. There is more than a distinctive touch of Vienna in the sweep of ring roads around the old city centre (*centro storico*) and broad avenues lined with imposing neo-classical buildings. Outsiders even observe something Viennese in the formal elegance of the Milanese bourgeoisie and their ceremonial attachment to La Scala, with all its pomp and grandeur.

The Milanese, of course, do not agree, and insist that they have a generally more dynamic attitude to life than their former Habsburg masters. Milan's intense activity is calmer, less chaotic than in some other large Italian cities. Indeed, the bustle here is almost orderly. Private cars are (nominally) forbidden in the tangle of narrow streets and small squares of the *centro storico*, making for a less fretful —and cleaner—environment.

Style is an essential part of the Milan ethos, and nowhere is it more apparent than in the superb shops on and around the Via Monte Napoleone, affectionately known as "Montenapo." Here, the pure genius of Italian design, whether it be in clothes or coffee pots, furniture or fountain pens, comes into its own. Even the football players of the town's two rival teams, AC and Inter Milan, dress like fashion models off the field.

Similar care goes into the cuisine of the city's many excellent restaurants, which benefit from the freshest produce of the surrounding rich farmlands of the Po Valley. Here, a risotto is not merely a stodgy rice dish, it's a poem.

The people themselves are a hard-working bunch. One third of Milan's population of 1.4 million is employed in industry, and the Milanese in general—who account for scarcely 3 percent of the national population—contribute one quarter of Italy's total income-tax revenues. This is a wealthy city; one look at the cluster of large factories in the northeastern suburbs around Sesto San Giovanni is enough to prove it.

Since World War II, the often dour temperament of the Lombards has been enlivened by the influx of sunnier Neapolitans and other southern immigrants. Those who work downtown can be seen at the magic hour of the *passeggiata,* the evening walk, strolling around the Piazza del Duomo,

Fashion Foremost

Despite the traumatic murders of two figureheads from top Milanese fashion houses, Maurizio Gucci in 1995 and Gianni Versace in 1997, Milan remains the fashion capital of the world. This is largely due to their proximity to the textile and silk mills in surrounding areas which supply the finest fabrics in the fashion industry. Gucci, Versace, Prada, and Armani boutiques pepper not only "Montenapo" but streets in Paris, Los Angeles, New York, and most other urban areas as well.

where conversation these days is less about politics than sport. After earning their daily bread, Milanese become frenetic football *tifosi* (supporters) at the Meazza Stadium, or impassioned Ferrari enthusiasts at the annual Formula One Grand Prix at Monza.

"La Dolce Vita"

The delight of Milan is not just the city itself, but the bonus of the surrounding countryside. Leave the city behind and escape to the lakes, a world apart where the waters lap the foothills of the Alps.

Lombardy's famous trio of elongated lakes—Maggiore, Como, and Garda—constitutes one of Europe's most romantic resort areas. Here you'll also find outstanding art museums in Bergamo and Brescia and, south of Milan, the Carthusian monastery of Certosa di Pavia—a jewel of late Gothic and Renaissance art. With vineyards, groves of orange and olive trees, atmospheric mists, craggy cliffs, and brilliant sun, the lakes are a home away from home for the poet, painter, and lover in us all.

Guarding the world's most coveted art collection is a man's—and a woman's—job.

A BRIEF HISTORY

Due to its strategic location at the heart of the Po valley, Milan has long been the "tough guy" of northern Italy. The first settlement in 600 B.C. was founded as the capital of the Insubres, a Celtic tribe from Gaul. Milan was known as *Mediolanum,* "town at the centre."

After conquest by the Romans in 222 B.C., Milan went on to become the major city of Cisalpine Gaul (Rome's Gallic lands south of the Alps). Under Emperor Augustus, it was second only to Rome itself. When the empire was split in two by Diocletian in the third century, Milan was declared the western emperor's residential and administrative capital, and rapidly proved a highly lucrative trading centre between Italy and northern Europe.

Ambrose, Attila, and the Lombards

It was a provincial governor, Aurelius Ambrosius, sent from Rome's German colony of Trier in A.D. 372, who placed Milan firmly on the European map. His reputation for justice and personal incorruptibility so sparked popular approval that he become bishop of Milan, and he is now known as St. Ambrose. Thanks to his scrupulous leadership and resistance to less than scrupulous emperors, Milan became a pillar of the Christian church.

Passing through the town in A.D. 452, Attila the Hun

A detail from the striking façade of Como's fifth-century Gothic-Renaissance cathedral.

showed little respect for Milan's spiritual values, offering a characteristic programme of rape and pillage. The Goths followed suit in A.D. 539, burning the city to the ground.

Some thirty years later, the Milanese clergy and their flock were on the run again, seeking the protection of Greek-led Byzantine forces around Genoa against the latest wave of invaders, the Lombards. Originally from north Germany, the *Langobardi* or Long Beards launched their attack on Italy from the Danube valley. Passing quickly through deserted Milan, rough, tough King Alboin established his court at Pavia, which he captured from the Byzantines in A.D. 572 after a three-year siege. He was murdered soon after, for forcing his wife to drink wine from the skull of her dead father.

To show the locals that they were not entirely barbarian, the Lombards set up courts of law, established an important school of jurisprudence at Pavia, and gradually abandoned their traditional system of vendetta. Their empire expanded through Italy as far down as the Duchy of Benevento, south of Naples.

The Lombards' most important king was one Liudprand (A.D. 712–744), who, in the interests of a tactical alliance with native Roman Catholics against the Byzantines, managed to persuade his fellow Lombards to give up the Arian heresy (see page 16) which they had brought from Germany.

By the time Charlemagne, king of the Franks, had conquered Lombardy, occupying Milan in A.D. 774, the people of Lombard and Roman stock had integrated to form what could be called the Italians.

The Middle Ages

In the ninth and tenth centuries, Milan bounced back. Once again, it was the church that boosted the city's self-confidence. Under energetic Archbishop Ansperto da Biassono, the city walls were rebuilt.

Historical Landmarks

600 B.C.	First settlement established by the Gauls.
222 B.C.	Conquest by the Romans.
3rd cen. A.D.	Mediolanum is capital of Western Roman Empire.
452	Attila the Hun plunders the city.
569	The Lombards invade, make Pavia their capital.
774	Charlemagne enters Milan, ending Lombard rule.
1045	Milan constitutes itself an autonomous commune.
1176	Lombard League defeats Barbarossa at Legnano.
1277	Ghibelline Visconti defeat Guelf Torriani at Desio Milan is Europe's largest city (pop. 200,000).
1351–1402	Gian Galeazzo Visconti starts Milan Cathedral.
1447–50	Ambrosian Republic.
1450–66	Francesco Sforza becomes Duke of Milan.
1466–99	Ludovico Sforza patronizes Leonardo da Vinci.
1499	King Louis XII of France seizes Duchy of Milan.
1535	Control seized by Charles V.
1540–1706	Spanish rule.
1706	Prince Eugene of Savoy installs Austrian regime.
1796–1814	Napoleon makes Milan capital of his Cisalpine Republic, then of the Kingdom of Italy (1805).
1814–59	Rise of the Risorgimento independence movement, against the restored Austrian regime. Austria is defeated at Marengo (1859).
1859	Milan heads Italy's industrial revolution.
1890s	First Socialist city government is elected.
1919	Mussolini founds the Fascist movement in Milan.
1939–45	World War II; Milan suffers heavy bombardment.
1960s–80s	Milan helps to revive Italian economy.
1993	Right-wing Lombard League mayor elected.
1994	Berlusconi's "Forza Italia" wins general election.
1995	Maurizio Gucci murdered in Milan.
1997	Gianni Versace murdered in Florida.
1998–2001	La Scala Opera House closed for renovation.

Observing a trait that was to become characteristic for the Milanese, a contemporary historian travelling through the city wrote of the people's "innate spirit of industry."

Trade soared, and the town soon showed off its prosperity by building two fine churches: Sant'Ambrogio and Sant'Eustorgio. The all-powerful Archbishop Ariberto da Antimiano (1018–1045), whose power and influence ranged far beyond Lombardy, gave Milan a national dimension. In 1045, the city declared itself a commune with autonomous government, and was vying for supremacy with its Lombard rivals, Pavia, Cremona, Lodi, and Como. (The latter two were crushed by Milan in fierce battles in the early 12th century.)

Attracted by this new power and wealth, Frederick Barbarossa ("Redbeard") looked to annex Milan in his Holy Ro-

Self-Made Saint

Aurelius Ambrosius (c. A.D. 334 or 340–397) was a no-nonsense bishop. Born of Christian parents but with no religious training, this Roman civil servant responded to his unexpected appointment by taking a crash course in theology. He was willing to "render unto Caesar" but not to let Caesar ride roughshod over his ideas of God. After his studies convinced him of the evil of Arianism (a heresy denying that Jesus was consubstantial with God), he refused the demand of Emperor Valentinian to hand over one of Milan's churches to the Arians. Emperor Theodosius I fell into line on this one, but when he massacred thousands of rebels in Thessalonica, Ambrosius not only excommunicated him but made him come to Milan and prostrate himself in penance at the cathedral. Of Theodosius, Ambrosius said: "the emperor is within the church; he is not above it."

man Empire. He smashed its city walls in 1162, but the Milanese forces resisted and the war continued until 1183. In the meantime, a new Lombard League was formed (1167) under Milan's leadership to repel the foreign invader.

Sirmione's Rocca Scaligera, on Lake Garda, was built by the Scaligeri lords of Verona.

On 29 May 1176, the Lombard League's troops, bearing the ferocious name of *Compagnia della Morte* (Company of Death), defeated Frederick Barbarossa's German forces at Legnano, northwest of Milan. The victory was vital for the national consciousness since for the first time the battle cry was heard for "the freedom and honour of Italy." (The battle was also cited in the electoral campaign of the revived Lombard League, which won the mayoral race in Milan in 1993.)

The ordinary citizens of Milan demanded rewards for their show of strength and valour on the battlefield. Guilds of workers in the wool and arms industries asserted their civic rights against the entrenched power of the church and aristocracy. Taxes, and contributions to church landowners, were reduced.

Rise and Fall of the Visconti

The 13th century ushered in the era of the great dynastic families. Some aristocrats decided that if they could not beat the people, they would join them—only at their head. The populist Torriani family, representing the Guelf faction (supporting the pope), led the Milanese in another, this time unsuccessful, battle against the German emperor, and lost the subsequent struggle for control of the city.

The Ghibelline forces (supporting the emperor) of Archbishop Ottone Visconti routed the Torriani at Desio in 1277.

With a family name derived from a hereditary 11th-century title of viscount, the archbishop was succeeded in 1295 by his great-nephew Matteo Visconti, who imposed a harsh, authoritarian rule over the commune and region. In gratitude for his military support, the German King Adolf of Nassau bestowed on him the title of Imperial Vicar of Lombardy. When this aroused the ire of Pope John XXII, Matteo (1250–1322) settled for *Signore* (Lord) of Milan. However, he did not escape excommunication on charges of heresy.

Milan prospered under the *signoria* (lordship) regardless. Its urban population of over 200,000 was the largest in Europe. Trade and industry—textiles and metalwork—boomed, and Matteo controlled Milan and much of Lombardy with an army of mercenaries; there were no communal forces to resist and the merchants were too busy making money to pay much attention to military matters. Enriched by lands outside Milan and ensured of the support of the German emperor, the Visconti had broken free of dependence on the hitherto demanding local populace. At the time, theirs was the most aggressive state in the whole of 14th-century Italy.

The Visconti were also great patrons of the arts, and in their time began building Milan cathedral, founded the Certosa (charterhouse) di Pavia, and made the University of Pavia one of the finest in Europe. Gian Galeazzo Visconti (1351–1402) was a disciple of the great poet Petrarch and ensured him a living by making him director of the Visconti library. He also developed a modern bureaucracy, conceiving state and government as a rationally planned "work of art." In 1395 he bought the title of Duke of Milan, for through an alliance with Isabelle de Valois he was about to marry into the French royal family. Their daughter, Valentina, married the French king's brother.

Gian Galeazzo's strong hold on power led him to ignore his nominal allegiance to the German emperor. He hired and fired officials at will, imposed taxes and laws without consulting the duchy's council, enforced mail-censorship, and controlled travel by introducing passports. The lands he expropriated at such strategically sensitive points gave him almost complete control of northern Italy, culminating in his seizure of Bologna in 1402. That same year, with his lordship already established over Pisa, Siena, and Perugia, he was poised to attack Florence when the plague providentially carried him off.

Visconti court etiquette had become highly refined and elaborate, effectively distancing the rulers from the people. Arbitrary tax-gouging and law enforcement characterized an authority dependent entirely on autocratic rule. Thus, under Gian Galeazzo's mad heir, Giovanni Maria, the Visconti empire quickly fell apart. By 1447, the dynasty had died out, though the female line passed through the Visconti to the Valois of France (notably Louis XII and François I, who were to stake claims to the duchy of Milan), as well as the Habsburgs of Austria and Spain, and the Tudors of England.

Renaissance under the Sforzas

The day after the death of the last Visconti despot, Filippo Maria, Milan established an "Ambrosian Republic." Born more of an unresolved power struggle between rival factions of aristocrats than of a popular movement for democracy, it proved unable to control its hinterland and lasted only three years before yielding to Francesco Sforza in 1450. The condottiere (captain) asserted his claim to the duchy as the husband of an illegitimate Visconti daughter, Bianca Maria.

The Sforza family had left their farms in Romagna, near Ravenna, to become mercenaries, offering their services in rapid succession to Ferrara, Naples, and Milan. The family name was adopted from a battle cry that can still be heard at Milan's football stadium and at the Italian Formula One races at Monza's Autodromo. When Francesco fell out with the Visconti, he joined the Medici of Florence and fought for

Leonardo the Plumber

As Renaissance men went, few could match the universal talents of Leonardo da Vinci (1452–1519), whose skills covered everything from mathematics and botany to aviation, sculpture, architecture and, on the side, a little painting. In 1482, when he left Florence for the court of Ludovico Sforza in Milan, his calling card was that of a musician. In his application for work, Leonardo himself listed his talents as a builder of cannons and fortifications, and master of piping for water and heat. He added as an afterthought: "I can carry out sculpture in marble, bronze or clay, and ... in painting I can do as well as any man."

During his 18 years in Milan, Leonardo spent most of his time as a glorified odd-job man around the Castello Sforzesco. In spare moments, he painted the *Last Supper* (1495–1497) at the church of Santa Maria delle Grazie, *Portrait of a Musician* at the Ambrosiana Library, the *Virgin of the Rocks* (c. 1483–1485) now hanging in the Louvre, and the *Litta Madonna,* now in the Hermitage in St. Petersburg. He also knocked off quick court commissions to portray Ludovico's mistresses, notably Cecilia Gallerani, which is now in Cracow.

them against Milan. Once installed as Duke of Milan, he actually formed an alliance with the Florentines against Venice and Naples.

Although no less despotic than the Visconti, the Sforza dynasty restored prosperity, particularly through expansion of the arms and silk industries, and brought a new artistic lustre to the city. With his son, Galeazzo Maria Sforza, Francesco built the splendid Ospedale Maggiore and restored the formidable Castello Sforzesco. His other son, Ludovico, completed the bulk of the work on the cathedral and built a great tribune for the Santa Maria delle Grazie and cloister for Sant'Ambrogio. He also expanded the network of canals for trade, and strengthened the city fortifications for defence against his enemies.

Deriving his nickname from his dark complexion and black hair, Ludovico il Moro ("the Moor") was politically less astute than his father but culturally the most brilliant of the Sforza dukes. He was a classical example of the Renaissance prince, ruthless in government, devious in diplomacy, and enlightened in his patronage of the arts. Among his protégés were the great architect Donato Bramante and Leonardo da Vinci. The glittering life of his court was famous throughout Europe.

Ludovico's lust for power pitted him against his mother in wresting the duchy from the rightful heir, his seven-year-old nephew, Gian Galeazzo, who had been "exiled" to a rival court in Pavia. Ludovico made and broke alliances with bewildering facility—first with Naples against Venice, then with France against Naples, and finally with Venice against France. He remained, however, relatively loyal to his father-in-law, the powerful Duke of Ferrara, and to the German emperor, Maximilian I, who had formally confirmed his right to the title of duke.

His machinations did get the better of him when, fearing trouble from Gian Galeazzo's followers, he encouraged the invasion by Charles VIII of France to seize the throne of Naples

"The Kiss," by Francesco Hayez, is hanging in Milan's Brera Museum.

in 1494. This fatal blunder marked the beginning of the end not only for the duchy itself, but also for all of Italy's independent city states.

Alarmed by the success of Charles VIII's military campaign, Ludovico then backed a Venice-led league to drive the French back out of Italy the following year. He emerged from the campaign as a short-term winner, boasting that Pope Alexander VI was now his chaplain, Emperor Maximilian his general, the Doge of Venice his chamberlain, and King Charles VIII his courier, but he had set in motion events that would prove his downfall.

In 1499, King Louis XII, grandson on his mother's side of Valentina Visconti, declared the Sforzas to be usurpers and marched into Milan to claim the duchy for himself. Tired of paying heavy taxes to support the luxury of the Sforza court and the cost of the wars, the Milanese cheered their new master. Ludovico attempted a comeback in 1500, but was roundly defeated and spent the rest of his life in exile, in the gilded prison of a Loire Valley château.

Foreign Rule

For the next 360 years, Milan was a pawn in the rivalries of the main continental European powers—Spain, France, and Austria. Under François I, the French vied with the Sforzas for control of Milan right until 1535, when Emperor Charles V seized the duchy for the Habsburgs. He ultimately handed it over to his son Philip, future king of Spain, in 1540; the Spanish subsequently ruled the city until 1706.

Unimaginative foreign rule and a series of plagues crippled Milan's economy. Among the few bright elements in two centuries of gloom were the forceful educational reforms of the city's archbishop, the enlightened Carlo Borromeo (1538–1584). (Conditions in this dark era of Milan's history are strikingly depicted in the celebrated novel of Alessandro Manzoni, *The Betrothed.*)

In 1706, during the War of Spanish Succession, the Habsburgs installed Prince Eugene of Savoy as governor to enforce Austrian administration. The city was slow to emerge from stagnation, but under a more efficient government in the second half of the 18th century, the economy began to pick up. At this time, wealthy merchants built the first of the Neo-Classical buildings that dominate the urban landscape. Cultural oppression, however, particularly in the form of censorship, drove writers and sociologists to form the *Società dei Pugni* (literally, Society of Fists), espousing the new ideas of the French Revolution.

After France's convincing defeat of the Austrians, Napoleon Bonaparte's soldiers were welcomed into the city as liberators in 1796. The Cisalpine Republic was proclaimed and the town boomed. In 1805, a grateful merchant bourgoisie applauded the republic's transformation into the Kingdom of Italy, with Milan as capital, and Napoleon crowned himself king in the cathedral.

Despite all the exactions of the French, Milan became the dominant force in Italian trade. It developed a proud new image, modernized by Napoleonic reforms in administration, scientific academies, and high-school education with French-style *lycées* for both boys and girls.

However, progress was halted by the collapse of the Napoleonic Empire and the return of conquering Austrian forces in 1814. Milan remained under Habsburg rule for another fifty years. Though eager to exploit the city's prosperity, the regime was as oppressive as ever. This time, imbued with a new self-assurance from contact with the French, the Milanese were not slow to resist. Poised at the forefront of the *Risorgimento* movement for national unity, the Milanese staged a revolt in

Napoleon in Milan

When Napoleon Bonaparte came to town, the Milanese cried: "Liberté, Egalité, Fraternité!" At a banquet in the Austrian archduke's palace, Napoleon told the city's gentry: "You will be free. Milan will be the national capital. You will have 500 cannons and France's eternal friendship." That same night, from his quarters in the Palazzo Serbelloni he wrote to Paris: "Don't worry, we'll get ten million francs from this place." Milan was then subjected to wholesale expropriations, plunder, taxes, and confiscation of art treasures from churches and private collections. Though most artworks were returned after the French defeat, some, like Titian's *Jesus Crowned with Thorns,* remain at the Louvre in Paris. It's only to fair to add, however, that Napoleon also founded Milan's Fine Arts Academy and the Brera Museum, which now house the retrieved booty.

Among the many things for which Napoleon was blamed, one was the weather. The genteel Milanese ladies told their darling French novelist, Stendhal, that it had never been so cold until that wicked man dug a road through the Simplon Pass, opening a hole in the hitherto protective Alpine barrier.

March 1848. They liberated the city for a glorious but brief four months before being brutally crushed by the Austrian army. Several streets and squares all over Lombardy are named after the five days—*Cinque Giornate*—of the uprising itself.

Following victory over the Austrians at Marengo in 1859, Vittorio Emanuele, the first king of independent Italy, entered the city with his French ally Napoleon III. They came in through the triumphal arch (now known as Arco della Pace), which had been designed for the French emperor's uncle 50 years earlier.

Thereafter, Milan remained in the vanguard of Italy's belated but dynamic industrial and commercial revolution. In the boom years, metal, chemical, and textile factories sprang up around the city's periphery, while publishing companies, banks, and the stock exchange dominated the centre. In the bold iron-and-glass roof of the Neo-Renaissance Galleria Vittorio Emanuele shopping arcade (see page 35), progress was given an architectural symbol. Leaving the political tangle to Rome, Milan was content with its role as the country's business capital.

Freedom and Fascism

At the turn of the 20th century, the city was a hotbed of radical political movement. It had elected its first Socialist mayor in the 1890s, and the Milanese newspapers, book publishers, and university had assembled Italy's most progressive minds.

In 1898, with the conservatives back in power, food riots protesting high wheat prices (essential for the daily pasta) led to the closure of the university and the presence of the army to enforce control. Its cannons left 100 dead and 600 wounded, including monks fired on by mistake when a crowd of beggars was waiting for soup outside their monastery.

This monument to Vittorio Emanuele II stands in the Piazza del Duomo.

It was in Milan in 1919 that Benito Mussolini founded his *Fasci Italiani di Combattimento* or Italian Combat League, known to history as the Fascists. In a hall lent by a circle of local merchants and industrialists, the ex-Socialist newspaperman assembled 60 anti-parliamentarians stirred by the ultranationalist sentiments of World War I. They started their campaign by shouting down Democrat speeches at La Scala, but quickly moved to more characteristic activities like burning the Milan headquarters of the Socialist newspaper, *Avanti!* After skillfully fanning the flames of the movement across the country, the *Duce* returned to Milan in 1922 to mastermind the March on Rome of 26,000 Blackshirts. So ended Italy's brief experience of democracy.

Fascism was an ambivalent and ultimately horrific experience for Milan. Archbishop Ildefonso Schuster and Monsignor Agostino Gemelli, rector of the Catholic University, proved enthusiastic supporters of the cause, but the town was also a principal centre of the anti-Fascist group *Giustizia e Libertà*.

In World War II, the city suffered 15 bombardments, the heaviest in 1943. The following year, Milan staged the nation's first general strike in protest against the war, leading to hundreds of workers being deported to German concentration camps. Fascist militia hanged 15 partisans on the Piazza

Loreto where, just nine months later, Fascist leaders themselves were executed by partisan firing squads, and the corpses of Mussolini and his mistress Clara Petacci were strung up—just a stone's throw from his own Milan monument, the Stazione Centrale.

After 1945, Milan has recovered quickly, taking a leading role in the country's economic miracle (but also in the crisis of confidence caused by the bribery scandals of the 1990s). Today it has the lion's share of Italy's major banks, its stock market and trade fairs, and is home to a range of heavy industries. In 1993, the discredited Socialist party, which for years had made the mayoralty its domain, gave way to the right-wing party of the Lombard League. In 1994, this was repeated in national elections, when the League, with Milan's TV-mogul Silvio Berlusconi's *Forza Italia* and the far right National Alliance Party (*Alleanza Nazionale*), the former neo-Fascist MSI party, gained the victory. But in the most recent elections, the leftist unity party L'Ulivo regained control of Milan's municipal government. The Milanese continue to devote themselves to what they do best: hard work.

Cold Shoulder

In January 1857, the crowds turned out for the Milan visit of Austria's Emperor Franz-Josef with his new bride Elizabeth ("Sissi") and greeted them not with violent demonstrations but with devastating silence. Fearing a boycott of the imperial couple's night at the opera at La Scala, the Austrians prepared to fill the boxes with their own people in borrowed evening wear. When obliged to say whether they would be using their subscription tickets, Milan's great families replied "yes" and then sent their servants instead.

WHERE TO GO

The region of Lombardy, covering Milan and the lakes, can be divided into five areas for sightseeing: the city of Milan itself; excursions to the nearby towns of Monza, Pavia, and Bergamo (all within day-trip distance if you want to keep Milan as your base); and the three lakes—from west to east, Maggiore, Como, and Garda.

MILAN

Even though it is not a sprawling metropolis like London or Rome, Milan is best taken in small doses. Start in the area around the Duomo (cathedral) and La Scala, taking time off for the shopping district of the Via Monte Napoleone, before visiting a couple of museums. Then, head for the Castello Sforzesco and its park before going on to Leonardo's *Last Supper*, his science museum, and Sant'Ambrogio Church.

Remember to keep at least half a day for the Brera Museum and the nearby galleries, and then take your pick from the other museums and churches. Don't forget to explore the city outskirts, and save plenty of time, too, just for relaxing: while away the hours on a café terrace in the artists' neighbourhood or Navigli canal district, and show the busy Milanese how to do something they often forget—the all-important *dolce farniente,* or the sweetness of doing nothing at all.

Most of Milan's major sights are within comfortable walking distance. The tram and bus system is rather difficult, but the subway (*Metropolitana Milanese*) is all you need.

Piazza Del Duomo

Few of the world's great cities have such an obvious focus for beginning a visit as the **Piazza del Duomo.** Designed by Giuseppe Mengoni, architect of the Galleria Vittorio

Lombardy Highlights

Milan. *Duomo Palazzo Reale, Piazza Duomo*: Architectural showpiece from the 14th century. Open 9:30 A.M. to 12:30 P.M., 3:00 to 6:00 P.M. Closed Monday. Metro: Duomo (see page 28).

Brera Museum, Via Brera 28: fine art collection, Academy of Fine Arts, National Library, and Astronomical Observatory. Open Tuesday through Saturday 9:00 A.M. to 5:30 P.M., Sunday and holidays 9:00 A.M. to 12:30 P.M. (See page 44)

Castello Sforzesco, Piazza Castello: Superb art in 14th-century castle. 9:30 A.M. to 5:30 P.M., closed Monday. Metro: Cairoli. (See page 38)

Last Supper, Piazza Santa Maria delle Grazie 2: Leonardo da Vinci's masterpiece, at the church of Santa Maria delle Grazie. 8:00 A.M. to 1:45 P.M., 2:00 to 6:30 P.M., closed Monday. Metro: Cadorna. (See page 42)

La Scala Opera House, Piazza della Scala: Possibly the world's most famous opera house. 9:00 A.M. to noon, 2:00 to 6:00 P.M. except national holidays. Metro: Duomo. (See page 35)

Navigli, Strada Alzaia Nzaviglio Grande: Regenerated area and artisans' haunt. Metro: Porta Genova. (See page 51)

Pavia. *Certosa di Pavia*: A 15th–century mausoleum and monastery. 9:00 to 11:30 A.M., 2:30 to 6:00 P.M. (closes 5:00 P.M. September and October, 4:30 P.M. in winter), closed Monday and national holidays. (See page 55)

Lake Maggiore. *Borromean Islands*: Baroque palazzo and tiered gardens on Isola Bella, and botanical gardens on Isola Madre. Palazzo open March through October 9:00 A.M. to noon, 1:30 to 5:30 P.M. (See page 64)

Lake Como. *Villa Serbelloni, Bellagio*: Splendid gardens and villa above Lake Como. Guided tours at 11:00 A.M. and 4:00 P.M., closed Monday. (See page 69)

Lake Garda. *Sirmione:* Village, spa, Roman ruins, and 13th–century castle. Castle open 9:00 A.M. to 1:00 P.M., 3:30 to 6:30 P.M. (9:00 A.M. to 2:00 P.M. winter), closed Monday. (See page 73)

The colours of the Duomo's grandiose marble façade are resplendent even on a grey day.

Emanuele, the square and arcades around the cathedral have for centuries provided a natural meeting place for both the Milanese and their pigeons.

As both geographical and psychological centre of Milan and the hub of the new Metro system, there is non-stop bustle during the day. This reaches its height at the magic moment of the *passeggiata,* when in the early evening people gather at the cafés, kiosks, and Portici Settentrionali arcade (running along the square's north side), dressed with casual elegance. The young make dates and discuss music and clothes, their fathers argue business and politics, and everybody else talks football.

The Cathedral

Milan's **Duomo** is the most grandiose of Italy's Gothic cathedrals. Begun in 1386 on the site of an earlier church (Santa Maria Maggiore), it took nearly six centuries to complete. The exterior of the cathedral has recently been completely restored, and the colours of the marble are resplendent, even on a grey Milan day.

Duke Gian Galeazzo Visconti founded the church as a votive offering to God in his plight to get himself a male heir. His plan worked, but his architectural demands proved too much for the local masons from nearby Lake Como, and French, Flemish, and German architects had to be called in to help. The major Italian contribution was by Pellegrino Tibaldi, who worked in the 16th century mainly on the interior, under the direction of revered Archbishop Carlo Borromeo (see page 23). The main spire was erected in the 18th century, the façade was completed under Napoleon in 1813, and work on other spires and exterior sculpture continued right up until the 20th century.

To best take in the bristling silhouette of marble pinnacles and statues and the awesomely flamboyant façade, stand on the south side of the cathedral in the courtyard of the Palazzo Reale. Despite the quite visible northern European influence, the Duomo presents a much broader and more "horizontal" appearance than most Gothic cathedrals of France and Germany.

Light through stained-glass windows colours the Duomo's interior as well.

Inside, the vast and noble space of the nave and four aisles shows more clearly the church's northern inspiration, particularly in the 52 soaring columns and the decoration of **stained-glass windows,** dating from the 15th century to the present day. The most precious stained glass, tracing the story of St. John the Evangelist, is to be seen in the south aisle (to the right). A 13th-century Visconti archbishop lies in the red marble sarcophagus mounted on pillars. In the right hand transept, notice the matter-of-fact treatment of an horrific martyrdom in Marco d'Agrate's 1562

There are more beautiful treasures from Milan's cathedral to be seen at the Museo del Duomo.

statue of St. Bartholomew: flayed alive, he is carrying his own skin.

A door to the right of the high altar leads down to the cathedral's **crypt,** where you can see an ancient reliquary and ivory carvings from the fourth and fifth centuries. The remains of Archbishop Carlo Borromeo are displayed here, draped in opulent finery.

Back in the north transept is the monumental 14th-century **Trivulzio Candelabrum,** with its seven branches of bronze.

Outside again, give yourself plenty of time for a spectacular walk out on the **roof** (where the profane cultivate a suntan). The elevator entrance (clearly signposted outside the Duomo) is in the south (right) transept. Wander high above the city, beneath the flying buttresses and around the statues (2,245 in all) and pinnacles (only 135), and climb up to the roof ridge for an unbeatable view of Milan. Make your way over to the apse at the rear of the roof for a close-up of the three magnificent Gothic windows. The intricately carved, white marble tracery and other roof sculpture are unique in Italian architecture.

(In the cathedral's west façade, a separate entrance leads to the octagonal, fourth-century **baptistery,** where St. Ambrose baptized St. Augustine in 387.)

Palazzo Reale

South of the cathedral (adjoining the main Tourist Office at the corner of Via Marconi), the **Palazzo Reale,** former residence of Milan's Spanish and Austrian governors, houses today the **Museo del Duomo** (Cathedral Museum). It displays Gothic sculpture from the cathedral exterior, a likeness of Gian Galeazzo Visconti, handsome 15th-century stained glass, Tintoretto's *Child Jesus with the Rabbis,* and a model of the Duomo as it was conceived in 1519.

Galleria Vittorio Emanuele II, Milan's grand 19th-century arcade.

On the palazzo's upper floor (access from the main courtyard) is the **Civico Museo di Arte Contemporaneo** (better known as CIMAC, Museum of Modern Art) with paintings by Giorgio Chirico, Giorgio Morandi, Filippo de Pisis, and the Futurists Carlo Carrà, Umberto Boccioni, Giacomo Balla, and Gino Severini. There is also sculpture by Lucio Fontana and Arturo Martini.

A quick walk farther south takes you over to the massive Renaissance **Ospedale Maggiore**, the main building of the University of Milan since 1958. Founded as a hospital by the Milanese Duke Francesco Sforza in 1456, the terracotta design of the right wing is by Antonio Filarete, architect of the Castello Sforzesco. Take a look inside at the grand central cloisters.

Piazza Mercanti

From the northwest corner of the Piazza del Duomo, take Via Mercanti, leading to the only medieval area in the city to have survived the devastating bombs of World War II and the wrecking ball of post-war building developers.

Before the cathedral was built, Piazza Mercanti was the centre of city life, with the seat of communal government, the Romanesque **Palazzo della Ragione** (1233), on its south side. Notice the fine equestrian relief of the 13th-century chief magistrate, Oldrado da Tressano, in a niche on the ground floor. The elegant upper storey was added in 1770. On the opposite side of the piazza, in black and white marble, is the Gothic **Loggia degli Osii** (from 1316) and the Baroque **Palazzo delle Scuole Palatine.**

Galleria Vittorio Emanuele II

Back on the north side of the Piazza del Duomo, through a triumphal arch, the massive, cross-shaped shopping arcade is a grand steel-and-glass vaulted monument to the expansive commercial spirit of the 19th century.

For cafés like the famous Zucca's, restaurants, boutiques, bookshops, and travel agencies, architect Giuseppe Mengoni provided an appropriate Neo-Renaissance décor—delightfully cool in summer, but a little draughty in winter. Sadly, a couple of days before the gallery's inauguration in 1878, Mengoni fell to his death from the roof.

La Scala Opera House

The Galleria offers a convenient passage from the Duomo to another holy of holies, La Scala—that 18th-century temple of musical drama, and probably the world's most celebrated opera house. (Its name is derived from the church it replaced, Santa Maria della Scala, which had been named after Regina della Scala, wife of a Visconti duke.) In contrast to the theatre's splendid galas, the façade is sober, even austere, perhaps because architect Giuseppe Piermarini did not want to compete with the brilliance of the carriages pulling up under his portico. Today, the BMWs and Ferraris have to drop off the Versace-robed ladies and their Armani-suited escorts at a slightly more respectful distance.

A display of puppets at the Museo Teatrale of La Scala Opera House.

Even if you cannot get tickets for a performance, you shouldn't miss the chance to visit the opera house via the **Museo Teatrale** (Theatre Museum), the entrance of which is under the portico to the left of the theatre proper.

Besides tracing the fascinating history of Milan opera and theatre with memorabilia of composers Verdi, Bellini, and Donizetti, the museum provides access to the auditorium. In six tiers, the red and gold horseshoe-shaped **opera house** seats 2,800 in 260 boxes, four balconies and the "gods" (see page 84 for more details). The opera house will be closed for restoration from 1998 to 2001.

Across the square from the theatre is Milan's handsome, 16th-century town hall, **Palazzo Marino,** and between them a totally undistinguished 19th-century monument to Leonardo da Vinci and his pupils.

Via Monte Napoleone

Only a few select shopping districts in the world achieve the status of monuments, and right up there with London's Bond Street, New York's Madison Avenue, Los Angeles's Rodeo

Drive, and Paris's Rue du Faubourg St. Honoré is what the Milanese know familiarly as "Montenapo."

Reached north of the Piazza La Scala along Via Alessandro Manzoni, the neighbourhood in which it lies is a veritable living exhibition of Milan's sense of modern and classical design at its very best. Fashion, jewellery, furniture, and luxurious household accessories are all on dazzling show along **Via Monte Napoleone** and **Via della Spiga,** not to mention the shops on the narrow streets between them.

Even if you're not buying, it is worth wandering among the elegant 18th-century palazzi housing boutiques with window displays that are works of art in themselves. Beyond the predominantly warm, yellow tones of the façades, explore the beautiful inner courtyards, which are wonderful havens of peace away from the city bustle. Nearby, everybody rushes on **Via Bagutta,** with its famous bistro of the same name (see page 137), **Via Sant'Andrea, Via Santo Spirito** and **Via Borgospessi** (see page 78).

Music In His Ears

On your way from La Scala along Via Alessandro Manzoni, notice at number 29 the Grand Hôtel de Milan, where Giuseppe Verdi died in 1901. Such is the veneration in which the composer is held in the Lombard capital, that Milanese legend insists that during his last days the street was strewn with straw to muffle the noise of passing horse carriages. Unfortunately, as the Italian saying has it, *Se non è vero, è ben trovato* ("If it's not true, it's a nice invention"). In fact, the considerate gesture was performed for an obscure Brazilian prince, Don Pedro II, ten years earlier, and Verdi's failing ears had to put up—even then—with the din of Milan traffic.

☛ Castello Sforzesco

The huge brick fortress northwest of the city centre (Metro: Cairoli) was rebuilt in its present form in the 15th century by Duke Francesco Sforza. It stands on the site of a Visconti castle destroyed by citizens of the short-lived Ambrosian Republic (see page 19). Used by the Spanish as a stronghold and by the Austrians as a refuge from the Italian uprising of 1848, it was converted to an art museum in the 1950s.

The four-square structure surrounds an interior courtyard, **Piazza d'Armi,** where fine summer concerts are held among the architectural fragments assembled here from other city monuments.

The main tower follows a Renaissance design by Florentine architect Antonio Filarete. Roman master Donato Bramante contributed part of the other work, with some interior décor—and plumbing (see page 20)—by Leonardo da Vinci.

The palace apartments were in the **Corte Ducale** over to the right, now the entrance to the **Musei del**

The funeral monument to Bernabò Visconti at Castello Sforzeco.

Castello (Castle Museums), which has a pioneering modern art display in an antique setting.

The *Arte Antiqua* collections of ancient and medieval art are devoted mostly to sculpture, notably including a Roman sarcophagus and some interesting statuary from Byzantine, Romanesque, and Gothic churches. Notice, too, the Gothic tombs of Bernabò Visconti, one of the more sadistically violent members of the Visconti clan, and his wife Regina della Scala—whose name survives in the opera house (see page 35).

The **frescos** in room 8, *Sala delle Asse,* in the northeast corner of the castle were done by Leonardo da Vinci but have since been badly damaged by over-restoration.

Room 15, *Sala degli Scarlioni,* is reserved for the Castello's Sforzeco's unfinished but still marvellous treasure, **Michelangelo**'s moving *Rondanini Pietà*. Named after its original home in the Palazzo Rondanini in Rome, it is a poignant, vertical treatment of Mary struggling to hold up the body of her crucified son.

Michelangelo worked on the piece on and off for nine years and was still chiselling away at it just six days before his death in 1564. There is a strange pathos in the great Renaissance master returning to Gothic forms for his last work in his 89th year. Nearby is a bronze bust of Michelangelo by his sculptor friend, Daniele da Volterra.

On the other side of the Corte Ducale, the **Pinacoteca** includes important paintings by Giovanni Bellini, Mantegna, Correggio, Titian, Lorenzo Lotto, Tintoretto, and Tiepolo. Local Lombard artists Foppa and Bergognone, and Leonardo's disciples Boltraffio and Sodoma are also represented.

Over in the **Rocchetta,** once the Palazzo's guards' room, are fine Egyptian and archaeological collections, as well as ceramics and furniture.

Parco Sempione

At the back of the Castello, the Sforza family's old hunting grounds were transformed at the end of the 19th century into delightful public gardens, carefully laid out as an English landscaped park.

The pace here is leisurely, away from the brisk bustle of the centre. In the right-hand corner of Parco Sempione is an **aquarium** of exotic tropical fish. Over on the left side of the park is the **Palazzo del Arte,** a thoroughly modern exhibition hall, most noted for the world famous *Triennale* show of decorative arts, which is held every three years.

A fine **equestrian statue** by Francesco Barzagli in the middle of the park flatters Napoleon III. It commemorates his passage through the **Arco della Pace** at the far end of the park, after the Italian-French victory over the Austrians in 1859 (see page 25). The triumphal arch is the starting point of the Corso Sempione, the Simplon Road that Napoleon Bonaparte ordered to be built through the Alps, whose presence reputedly influenced local climatic conditions (see page 24).

Leonardo's Milan

Leonardo spent 18 years in the service of Duke Ludovico Sforza (see page 20), and several monuments testify to the artist's presence in the city.

From the west side of the Castello Sforzesco (Metro: Cadorna), you are within easy walking distance of two monuments which demonstrate the different sides of Leonardo da Vinci's genius—his acclaimed artistic masterpiece, the *Last Supper,* in part of the old Dominican monastery (see opposite and page 42), and his scientific inventions in the science museum (see page 43). The church of Sant'Ambrogio, Milan's most venerated place of worship, is conveniently nearby.

Even without Leonardo da Vinci's painting in the adjoining building, the church of **Santa Maria delle Grazie** (on Via Caradosso) would be worth a visit as a jewel of Renaissance architecture. Adding to an earlier Gothic design, in 1492 Donato Bramante—Pope Julius II's chief architect in

Autopsy of a Masterpiece

The great culprit in the disintegration of the *Last Supper* (1498) was not so much the Milanese humidity or pollution as Leonardo himself—or at least the impossible demands of his genius.

For this pinnacle of his life's work, Leonardo da Vinci wanted to avoid the restrictions of fresco painting on damp plaster, which had to be done section by section and could not be modified once the paint had dried. This would have denied him the chance to add the shadowy *sfumato* effect that helps to give his paintings their psychological depth and subtlety. Additionally, the sustained effort demanded by damp plaster would have meant that he could not—as was his custom—leave the painting when inspiration deserted him to go and work on something else.

So Leonardo used instead his own concoction of tempera with oil and varnish on a dry surface—a disastrous choice for the humid climate. Deterioration of the painting was noted as early as 1517, when the great master was still alive. By the time fellow artist Giorgio Vasari saw it one generation later, there was "nothing visible but a muddle of blots." It's a miracle that 400 more years of candle smoke, damp, dust, and smog have left anything at all.

Rome—fashioned a magnificent red brick and white stone **chancel** (*tribuna*) towering over the rear of the church. The graceful lines of the rectangular choir and 16-sided cupola are best viewed from the little **cloister** that Bramante built on the north side. Once inside the church—which was originally conceived as the Sforza family's burial place (the tombs of Ludovico il Moro and his wife Beatrice are to be restored to their rightful place here)—stand in the choir to appreciate the full majesty of the chancel's dome.

Notice, too, the exquisite inlaid wood and carving of the prayer stalls in the apse.

Leonardo da Vinci's **Last Supper** (*Cenacolo*, 1498) is still on view even though it is being lovingly resuscitated in the little Dominican refectory to the left of the church. Despite centuries of deterioration and clumsy restoration

The restoration of da Vinci's "Last Supper" continues, as does the stream of visitors eager to view the masterpiece.

since it was completed, it still carries enormous psychological impact. In the moment Leonardo has chosen to capture in his painting, we see the trauma of each of the disciples following Jesus' declaration: "One of you will betray me."

Almost as awe-inspiring as the painting itself is the painstaking, inch-by-inch recovery of the fragmentary but still powerful traces of the "real Leonardo." Now nearly complete, this recovery work has been underway since 1979. The results reveal, for example, that Philip (third to the right, leaning over towards Jesus) has an expression of acute grief, not the simpering pathos left by "restorers" who presumed to improve on the original.

On the wall opposite, the superb condition of Donato da Montorfano's *Crucifixion* (dating from 1495) shows how much better preserved Leonardo's work would have been if he had only accepted the constraints of fresco—but the *Last Supper* would then perhaps have been less emotionally inspired as a painting.

For the other aspect of Leonardo's talents—just as fascinating—visit the **Museo della Scienza e della Tecnica** (Science and Technology Museum) in the nearby Via San Vittore. Among the rooms devoted to scientific history, one gallery is reserved for **Leonardo's inventions.** They are displayed as models, constructed from details in his notebooks. You will see his aircraft, a machine for making screws, a revolving bridge, an hydraulic timber-cutter, some machine-tools, and a system of map-making by aerial views long before any aircraft, even his own, had become operational.

The Church of Sant'Ambrogio

At the eastern end of Via San Vittore, beyond a noble atrium, Milan's most revered sanctuary, dedicated to the city's patron saint, was built between the ninth and 12th centuries. It stands on the site of a church built in A.D. 386, founded by Aurelius Ambrosius, first Bishop of Milan, along with Peter, Paul, and Jerome (see page 16). Its position, next to the Catholic University, honours the scholarship of the man who left a revered personal legacy of hymns and philosophical homilies.

The sober, five-bayed façade is characteristic Lombard Romanesque, flanked by a ninth-century campanile on the right and a taller 12th-century tower to the left, and topped by a modern loggia.

In the interior, left of the handsome rib-vaulted nave, notice the 11th-century **pulpit** standing over a Christian sarcophagus of the Roman era. In the north (left) aisle are Bergognone's painting of *Jesus the Redeemer* and Bernardino Luini's *Madonna*, in the south (right) aisle, frescos by Tiepolo. The **high altar,** covered in gold and silver and richly embedded with precious stones, stands beneath a ninth-century canopy carved with Byzantine-Romanesque reliefs.

Key question words:
***Quando* (kwahndoa) – When?**
***Chi* (kee) – Who?**

The remains of St. Ambrose himself are buried in the **crypt** beneath the presbytery at the far-east end of the church. The nearby church **museum** displays early Christian mosaics, medieval sculpture, and frescos by Bergognone and Luini.

The Brera

Just a short walk east of the Castello Sforzesco, the handsome 17th-century palace of the Jesuits today houses the **Pinacoteca di Brera,** one of Italy's foremost art museums, with an unrivalled collection of northern-Italian painting.

In its fine arcaded courtyard, notice a bronze statue of Napoleon—a remarkable, rare example of the emperor with no clothes. (The marble original is at Apsley House, London.) Homage is paid here to Napoleon Bonaparte for turning the Brera into a national gallery with the art he confiscated from the Church and recalcitrant nobles. Most of what he expropriated in Italy for the Louvre in Paris ended up back in Milan at the Brera after Waterloo.

Giuseppe Feliza da Vollpedo's "Fiumana" at the Pinacoteca di Brera.

Among the highlights are: paintings by Giovanni Bellini of the *Madonna and Child* and an exquisitely personal *Pietà;* two Titian portraits, *Antonio Porcia* and *St. Jerome;* Veronese's *Jesus in the Garden;* Tintoretto's dramatic *Discovery of St. Mark's Body;* and an impressive *Jesus at the Column* by the many-talented Donato Bramante.

Mantegna's works include a touching *Madonna,* but his masterpiece here is the *Dead Jesus,* which achieves a gripping emotional effect. Piero della Francesca's celebrated *Montefeltro Altarpiece* (1474) was his last work.

The ethereal beauty of Correggio's *Nativity* and *Adoration of the Magi* and Raphael's stately *Betrothal of the Madonna* contrast with the earthier inspiration of Caravaggio's *Supper at Emmaus.*

Lombard masters include Bergognone, Boltraffio, Foppa, and Luini, while the non-Italian artists represented include El Greco, Rubens, Van Dyck, and Rembrandt. The modern collection has good works by Modigliani, Boccioni, de Chirico, Carrà, and de Pisis.

The Artists' Quarter

Immediately west of the Pinacoteca di Brera, artists and antiques dealers alike vie for the high-rent galleries and shops along **Via Fiori Chiari** and **Via Madonnini** and around the **Piazza Formentini**.

Not many can afford the wares at the very chic **flea market** that takes place on the third Saturday of each month, but the Italian national sport of people-watching is cheap enough, so just stroll around the neighbourhood and then find a table for the price of an espresso at one of the neighbourhood's smart, lively cafés.

Other Museums and Churches

Museo Poldi-Pezzoli

This museum on Via Alessandro Manzoni 12 has the charm of a formerly private collection, which contains not only splendid paintings, but also antique watches, sundials, and fine 16th-century Persian carpets, as well as soldiers' chain mail armour and face masks.

Among the masterpieces of its paintings are a Giovanni Bellini *Pietà*, Piero della Francesca's *San Nicola da Toledano*, Mantegna's *Madonna and Child*, a Botticelli *Madonna*, Antonio Pollaiuoli's lovely *Portrait of a Young Woman* and important works by Palma Vecchio, Filippo Lippi, Perugino, Lorenzo Lotto, Tiepolo, and the Lombard masters.

Biblioteca Ambrosiana

Situated on Piazza Pio XI, 2, the Ambrosiana recently has been thoroughly renovated. Its great library was originally housed in the 17th-century palace of Cardinal Federigo Borromeo (nephew of the great Italian churchman, Archbishop Carlo Borromeo; see page 23). Among its precious manuscripts are

Museum Highlights

(See Lombardy Highlights on page 29.) Opening hours should be confirmed at local tourist information offices (see page 126).

Milan. *Ambrosiana*, Piazza Pio XI 2; tel. 806 921: Paintings housed in a 17th-century library. 9:30 A.M. to 5:00 P.M., closed Saturday. Metro: Cordusio. Currently closed for restoration. (See page 46)

Archeologico, Corso Magenta 15; tel. 8645 0011: Greek, Etruscan, and Roman antiquities. 9:30 A.M. to 5:30 P.M., closed Monday. Metro: Cadorna. (See page 48)

Science (*Scienza e Tecnica*), Via San Vittore 21; tel. 485 551: Leonardo's inventions. Tuesday through Friday 9:30 A.M. to 5:00 P.M. (until 6:30 P.M. Saturday and Sunday), closed Monday. Metro: Sant'Ambrogio. (See page 43)

Teatrale, Piazzale della Scala 2; tel. 8905 3418: La Scala opera. 9:00 A.M. to noon, 2:00 to 6:00 P.M. (closed Sunday November through April) (see page 36).

Pavia. *Castello Visconteo*, Piazza del Castello: City art museum. 9:00 A.M. to 12:15 P.M., closed Monday and afternoons. (See page 59)

Bergamo. *Accademia Carrara*, Piazza Carrara: Venetian and Lombard art. 10:30 A.M. to 12:30 P.M., 4:30 to 8:30 P.M. (10:30 P.M. Thursday), 10:30 A.M. to 8:30 P.M. Saturday and Sunday, closed Tuesday. (See page 64)

Lake Como. *Tempio Volta*, Giardini Pubblici, Viale Marioni, Como: Electricity pioneer's scientific instruments. 10:00 A.M. to noon, 3:00 to 6:00 P.M. April through September, 10:00 A.M. to noon, 2:00 to 4:00 P.M. October through March. (see page 70).

Lake Garda. *Pinacoteca Tosio-Martinengo*, Piazza Moretto, Brescia: Renaissance masters. 9:00 A.M. to noon, 2:00 to 5:00 P.M., closed Monday, Friday; Saturday 9:00 A.M. to noon, Sunday 2:00 to 5:00 P.M. (See page 75)

Leonardo da Vinci's drawings, which illustrate his scientific and artistic theories.

The Ambrosiana's superb art gallery boasts as one of its most precious treasures Leonardo's luminous *Portrait of a Musician* (1485), unfinished but the best preserved of the master's few surviving works. You can see his pervasive influence on Milanese artists in the decorative paintings of Bernardino Luini and in the *Portrait of a Young Woman* by artist Ambrogio de Predis.

San Lorenzo Maggiore's sixteen Corinthian columns are the last of Milan's Roman remains.

There's nothing sweet about Caravaggio's *Bowl of Fruit*—the worm is already in the apple and the leaves are withering. Titian is also well represented at the Ambrosiana, notably with an imposing *Adoration of the Magi.*

One of the most fascinating exhibits, however, particularly for those who know Raphael's great *School of Athens* fresco in the Vatican, are the great Renaissance master's so-called "cartoons"—his preparatory drawings for the piece.

Museo Archeologico

Situated on Corso Magenta 15, the archaeological museum harbours a collection of Greek, Etruscan, and Roman antiquities—namely sculpture, sarcophagi, and ceramics—in the disused 16th-century **Monastero Maggiore** (entrance is through the cloisters). In the monastery's lay chapel there are several frescos by artist Bernardino Luini.

Museo di Milano

The municipal museum, on Via Sant'Andrea 6, in the 18th-century Palazzo Morando, traces the city's history through a series of paintings, drawings, and prints. The specific history of Italy's independence movement in the 19th century is recounted in the **Museo del Risorgimento** (Via Borgonuovo 23).

San Satiro Church

Standing off the busy Via Torino near the Ambrosiana library (see page 46), San Satiro is a major work of Renaissance modelling (1478) by Donato Bramante. Walk round to Via Falcone to view its fine exterior, the 11th-century campanile, and newly restored **Cappella della Pietà.** The handsome interior has a characteristic Milanese décor of terracotta. A Greek cross space is created by an optical illusion. Over the high altar is a 13th-century *Madonna and Child* fresco. Notice, too, the elegant, Renaissance, octagonal **baptistery** off the south (right) aisle.

Signs:
entrata **– entrance**
uscita **– exit**
arrivo **– arrival**
partenza **– departure**

Church of San Lorenzo Maggiore

San Lorenzo Maggiore is situated south of the city centre, near the ancient **Porta Ticinese,** and the sixteen Corinthian columns from a temple portico, which together comprise Milan's only substantial Roman remains. With its late 19th-century façade, the Romanesque church stands on the site of an early Christian church founded in the fourth century.

To mark that era is a striking bronze statue (recast) of Emperor Constantine.

San Lorenzo's outstanding feature, on the south (right) side, is the octagonal **Chapel of Sant'Aquilino** built in the fourth century as an imperial mausoleum. Inside are fifth-century mosaics of Jesus, the Apostles, and Elijah, an early Christian sarcophagus, and Roman architectural fragments.

Sant'Eustorgio Church

A park, **Parco delle Basiliche,** stretches south of San Lorenzo Maggiore down to the medieval **Sant'Eustorgio.** This graceful church was started in the 11th century and harmoniously added to over the next 400 years. Notable additions are the fine **campanile** and the **Capella Portinari,** a true jewel of Renaissance architecture. The chapel, which is visited separately (for a donation), is dedicated to St. Peter the Martyr, a 13th-century inquisitor murdered by one of his victims and honoured here with masterly frescos (1468) by Vincenzo Foppa.

Key question words:
What? – ***Che cosa***
(kay kawsah)
Where? – ***Dove***
(doavay)

Just as impressive is the inquisitor-martyr's **tomb** sculpted by Giovanni di Balduccio in 1339. Also off the south (right) transept, the gigantic Roman sarcophagus in the **Chapel of the Magi** contained the relics of the three kings until 1164, when they "followed yonder star" to Cologne.

Church of Santa Maria presso San Celso

Santa Maria presso San Celso, on Corso Italia, is a Romanesque church with a 10th-century bell-tower. Visit it on a bright day, in order to view Paris Bordone's beautiful *Holy Family with St. Jerome* and 14th-century frescos, both in the south (right) aisle, as well as the handsome inlaid-wood

choir stalls. In the north (left) aisle is Bergognone's *Jesus in the Stable.*

Away from the City Centre

So many of Milan's churches, monuments, and museums are concentrated inside the periphery bounded by the Castello Sforzesco and Ospedale Maggiore that few visitors venture outside. The following are some of the sights worth exploring outside the city centre.

Navigli Canal District

Once a modest but colourful working-class neighbourhood on the south side of town, the *Navigli* district has become popular for its bars, bistros, open-air cafés, boutiques, galleries, and artists' studios.

Two canals start out from the **Darsena basin** near the sprawling Piazza XXIV Maggio (where a pompous arch cel-

A sign of the city's prosperity, the old Navigli canals are now a chic bourgeois neighourhood.

ebrates Napoleon III's victory over the Austrians at Marengo; see page 25). The **Naviglio Grande** runs west out to Abbiategrasso, and the **Naviglio Pavese** south to Pavia. They were originally dug in the Middle Ages to bring agricultural products into the city, and by the 17th century they also served the gentry as waterways to their country villas.

From May to mid-September guided cruises are offered on the Naviglio Grande; for more details, contact the Milan Tourist Office (see page 126). A popular local festival is held here on the first Sunday in June (see page 79).

Giardini Pubblici

Just north of the city centre, the private gardens of the 18th-century aristocracy have been transformed into a delightful 17-hectare (42-acre) public park. Wide avenues of chestnut trees crisscross handsome landscaped gardens in the classical Italian style, rockeries, and duck ponds.

For children, there is a host of pony-carts, a miniature train, and nippy dodgem cars: a great relief from Milan traffic stress.

Inside the park, the classical French-style **Villa Reale,** built in 1793 for the Belgioioso family, has an art collection of Italian futurists (the Italian movement that arose in 1909 and included Boccioni, Carrà, and Balla), sculpture by Marino Marini, and French 19th-century artists (among others Corot, Sisley, Manet, Cézanne, Gauguin, and Van Gogh).

The **Museo di Storia Naturale** (Natural History Museum), the largest in Italy, has a great collection of minerals, giant crystals, insects, fossils, and dinosaurs, as well as a library. Alternatively, you can always reach for the stars at the nearby **Planetarium.**

On the far-west side of the park, in the Palazzo Dugnani, the **Cinema Museum** shows old cameras, projectors, and, best of all, films.

The Stazione Central's steel vaulting expresses the city's commercial and industrial dynamism.

Stazione Centrale

Mussolini's promise to make the trains run on time found its architectural expression in Italy's largest railway station. Stazione Centrale's imposing mass and monstrous bombast is the perfect epitome of fascist design (1925–1931).

But, even if you're not taking a train, have a peek inside. Compared with the aggressive façade, the interior is much more successful. It is built on a gigantic scale and designed to impress, but achieves its effects with panache, notably in the steel-and-glass vaulting over the platforms.

The man who inflated its neo-classical forms was Ulisse Stacchini. Fortunately, architects Giò Ponti and Pierluigi Nervi were around in the fifties to offset the damage with their sleekly elegant **Pirelli Building** (or *Grattacielo Pirelli*, the first skyscraper in Italy), which looks down on the station from across the Piazza Duca d'Aosta.

This 127-metre- (416-foot-) high tower, 25 metres (80 feet) in length, was erected to mark the site of Pirelli's first of many rubber factories and is now the seat of government for the whole region of Lombardy. With its graceful sides tapering like a ship's bow, it was among the very first skyscrapers to abandon the standard, rectangular block design, using, instead, a revolutionary hexagonal structure.

***fumatori* – smoking**
***non fumatori* – non-smoking**

☛ *Cimitero Monumentale*

Not everyone thinks of a cemetery as a place to go sightseeing. This particular resting place, however, is well worth the 15-minute taxi ride northwest of the Duomo for its amazing tributes in granite and marble to bourgeois Milanese pride and pathos.

When they say *monumentale*, they are not kidding. A Pharaonic pyramid, enormous Roman sarcophagus, lifesize crucifixion, and several other morbid but fascinating tributes vie for your attention—nothing, it seems, is too good for the dearly departed Milanese. The centrepiece is a gigantic Neo-Gothic temple sheltering the tomb of novelist Alessandro Manzoni, author of *I promessi sposi (The Betrothed),* along with busts of the revered Verdi—who wrote his *Requiem* in honour of Manzoni—and independence heroes Giuseppe Garibaldi and Camilo Cavour.

Soldiers are particularly well served, including a colonel sculpted with all his medals and a sergeant major being devoured by a Gorgon. Best of all is one Davide Campari who, before he died, commissioned a full size reproduction of Leonardo's *Last Supper* for his tomb. The guardians are usually pleased to show you where.

CITY EXCURSIONS

Although the towns of Pavia, Monza, and Bergamo can all be reached on easy day trips from Milan, they also make for good overnight trips. Bergamo, in particular, is a very pleasant stopover on the way to or from Lake Garda.

Certosa di Pavia

After the Milan Duomo itself, this great charterhouse, begun in the 15th century as a Visconti family mausoleum, is the most spectacular monument in the region. A 30-

There's Italian city life to be sampled in other towns outside of Milan proper.

minute drive south of Milan, it can be visited independently of Pavia itself, which lies 10 km (6 miles) farther down the road.

Beyond the public entrance, the interior courtyard leading to the church has **wine cellars** and **food stores,** across from the Baroque **Palazzo Ducale,** which constitutes the prior's and ducal apartments.

For the monastery's church, Duke Gian Galeazzo Visconti used many of the masons and sculptors who were working on his cathedral in Milan (see page 18). The edifice marks a crucial point in the transition in styles from flamboyant Gothic to Renaissance. Even without the originally designed crowning gable, the sculpted marble **façade** has a dazzling impact. There are more than 70 statues of prophets, saints, and apostles above the medallion reliefs of Roman emperors.

The Gothic interior, with its groin vaulting, is lightened by some brightly coloured paving. Among the chapels, which were decorated in Baroque style in the late 16th century, notice in the north (left) aisle an exquisite Perugino altarpiece of *God the Father*. Right of the triumphant Baroque high altar are a finely carved 15th-century *lavabo* (ritual basin) and a charming *Madonna and Child* by Bernardino Luini. In the south (right) transept is the **Visconti tomb.**

A door here leads to a small cloister of terracotta offering a good view of the church's galleried octagonal tower. The **Great Cloister** farther to the south boasts 122 arches, with similar terracotta decoration for the monks' 24 cells. In 1947, Cistercian monks took over from the Carthusians; fortunately, they have continued the traditional manufacture of herbal liqueurs. Their **refectory** has glorious ceiling frescos by Bergognone.

Pavia

The Lombards' first capital is now a sleepy, red-brick university town (population 100,000), some 34 km (21 miles) south of Milan. Hurry through its modern suburbs to the attractive *centro storico*.

The Lombard kings established their court in Pavia in the sixth century (see page 14); French King Charlemagne was crowned Emperor here in 774, Frederick Barbarossa in 1155; and this was the birthplace (c. 1005) of Lanfranc, first Archbishop of Canterbury under the Normans. The French have less happy memories of the city, since King François I was captured by Emperor Charles V in 1525 at the crucial battle of Pavia (in the northern outskirts at Mirabello) and imprisoned in Madrid.

The Spanish ramparts from the 17th century are visible along the northern edge of the city centre as you drive in from Milan. Start walking on the south side of town at the **Ponte Coperto** (Covered Bridge), which spans the Ticino river. It has been reconstructed east of the medieval original, which was

University students in Pavia have a long and proud tradition to live up to.

The 18th-century Villa Mirabello in Varese is home to the Museo Civico (municipal museum).

bombed in 1944. The Ticino descends from Switzerland via Lake Maggiore to join the Po southeast of Pavia.

From the picturesque riverside road, take the Via Diacono over to the **Church of San Michele,** the city's major Romanesque monument. Its octagonal dome was completed in 1155 for Emperor Frederick Barbarossa's coronation. The simple sandstone façade is notable for its subtly sculpted friezes over the three recessed portals and an elegant band of 21 arches following the angle of the roof gable. The interior has superb rib-vaulting over the nave and aisles and fine carving on the column capitals.

Head left on Corso Garibaldi and turn right along Strada Nuova, which traces the old Roman road's south-north axis from the Ponte Coperto. Behind the *Broletto* (town hall) is the late-15th-century **Duomo,** a Renaissance structure with details added by Bramante and Leonardo da Vinci. The dome dates from the 19th century but the façade was not completed until later, in 1933.

Back on Strada Nuova, cross the ancient Roman east-west axis (now Corso Mazzini and Corso Cavour), to pass the 18th-century buildings of the **University of Pavia,** on the right. The university was originally founded by the Lombards as the nation's foremost school of law, and was made a full university by the Visconti in 1361. Pavia's most celebrated teacher was Alessandro Volta (1745–1827), professor of physics and pioneer in electricity who gave his name to the unit of electric measurement. Napoleon bestowed on him the title of count.

A well conceived **museum** recounts the fascinating history of the university. On Piazza Leonardi da Vinci are three medieval **tower houses** of the Pavia nobility and beneath the square the 11th-century **crypt** of Sant' Eusebeio.

At the north end of Strada Nuova is the Visconti's formidable 14th-century fortress, **Castello Visconteo.** Its rear fourth side was lost in 1527, but there are two corner turrets remaining on the south side. Enter the fine terracotta arcaded courtyard for access to the **Museo Civico** (see page 68). Besides a small but interesting collection of Roman antiquities and Lombard sculpture, the **Pinacoteca** houses important works by Giovanni Bellini, Correggio, Boltraffio, Foppa, Tiepolo,

Monza is the home of Grand Prix racing and more casual forms of transportation as well.

and the Netherlands painters Hugo Van der Goes and Lucas Van Leyden.

Over to the west (at the end of Via Griziotti), the 12th-century church of **San Pietro in Ciel d'Oro** is revered as the last resting place of St. Augustine, whose relics are said to have been brought here from Carthage (near where he died in 430) and are now enshrined in the great Gothic, sculpted marble **Arca di Sant'Agostino** (1362). The Romanesque interior provides a simple setting for the grandiose monument. The *Ciel d'Oro* (golden ceiling) of the church's name refers to a now long-gone gilded vault. A verse from Dante's *Paradiso* is quoted on the façade in reference to the martyred Roman poet Boethius, who is buried in the crypt.

Monza

If you do not feel like driving through Milan's northeast industrial suburbs, it's an easy 20-minute bus ride from beside the Stazione Centrale to the fabled home of Grand Prix motor racing (see page 86). Don't forget that there is more to the town than just high-speed maniacs, however, and that the friendly population of 120,000 is also involved in manufacturing hats and carpets.

The track and grandstands take up some 15 percent of the lovely **Villa Reale park,** which covers 800 hectares (2,000 acres) in all. The land was confiscated from the aristocracy and handed over to the people in 1805 by Napoleon's stepson and viceroy in Italy, Eugène de Beauharnais. The English-style landscaped parkland is still dotted with patrician mansions and is home to the Austrian Archduke Ferdinand's Neo-classical Villa Reale (1780), which stands among rose gardens and greenhouses.

This is great picnic country and caters for every manner of sport—tennis, golf (Milan Golf Club has 18- and 9-hole courses), polo, grass hockey, swimming, skating, hiking, and jogging. Bicycles can also be rented in the park. Wild stag, hare, and pheasant roam freely, some all the way onto the woodlands in the middle of the racetrack. Horse races are held at the Mirabello hippodrome.

Historically, Monza was an important city of the Lombard kings. The Gothic **cathedral** is older than Milan's, and is notable for its 13th-century white-and-green marble façade, rose-window and Pellegrino Tibaldi's brick campanile (1605). The church was founded in A.D. 595 by the Lombard Queen Theodolinda, whose tomb is in a chapel to the left of the high altar. In the church's **Museo Serpera,** downstairs beneath the north aisle is the Lombards' **Iron Crown**—as used in the coronation both of Holy Roman Emperors and

Farewell to Arms

Bartolomeo Colleoni (1400–1476) was so successful a *condottiere* that the problem for his masters was how to stop him. Born of an aristocratic family just outside Bergamo, he signed on as a soldier in 1419 in southern Italy, notably under Muzio Attendolo, founder of the Sforza dynasty and father of the future Duke Francesco Sforza of Milan. He came north again to fight for the Venetians in 1431 against the Visconti at Cremona.

Continuing to fight the Milanese until 1448, Colleoni then rejoined the Sforza family, who had by then formed an alliance with Venice. The unabashed machismo of his coat of arms, a pun on the family name—*coglioni,* a pair of testicles—says it all. The Venetian Republic made him commander-in-chief but relieved him of active duty. Colleoni spent his last years close to Bergamo at his favourite residence, the Castle of Malpaga, surrounded by painters, men of letters and soldiers.

Napoleon himself (as king of Italy; see page 23). It is said to contain a piece of iron beaten from one of the nails used to hammer Jesus to the cross. Theodolinda's treasure also includes ancient silver, ivory, embroidery, silk, and other religious relics.

Bergamo

Rising out of the plain of the Po valley around its own steep little hill, roughly 47 km (30 miles) northeast of Milan, the delightful town of Bergamo makes a welcome break in the monotony of the *autostrada*. Divided into lower and upper cities (*Città Bassa* and *Alta* respectively), the population of 122,000 earns a living from clothes manufacturing and the metal industry. It has a proud soldiering history, having given the Venetian Republic a famous *condottiere,* Bartolomeo Colleoni, and the largest contingent in Garibaldi's 1,000 Red Shirts for the *Risorgimento* (see opposite). A funicular links the two parts of the city.

Fuel types:
unleaded – *senza piombo*
regular – *normale*
premium – *super*
diesel – *gasolio*

Città Bassa

The Lower City is the modern town of shops, hotels, and restaurants—serving a savoury *risotto* which they insist is superior to Milan's. As it is today, the area was laid out with style and panache in the early 20th century along airy, broad boulevards and squares by Marcello Piacentino, before he succumbed to the demands of Mussolini as official architect of the Fascist state.

The main street, Viale Giovanni XXIII, leads to Piazza Matteotti and the hub of the town's lively café scene along the tree-lined **Sentierone** arcades. Opposite is the 18th-century **Teatro Donizetti** and a monument showing the Bergamo-born opera composer accompanied by the naked lady he is always said to have needed for inspiration.

At the eastern end of the piazza, step inside the church of **San Bartolomeo** to look at Lorenzo Lotto's fine altar painting (1516). Climbing to the Upper City, farther east, **Via Pignolo** is most notable for its elegant 16th- to 18th-century palazzi and the church of **Santo Spirito,** with a fine polyptych by Bergognone.

Città Alta

Venetian ramparts still protect the historic Upper City on the 366-metre- (1,200-foot-) tall hill. "Alta," meaning "high," refers to the city's altitude, 400 metres (1,300 feet) above sea level. The gracious **Piazza Vecchia** is surrounded by a vast number of Renaissance public edifices—notably the **Palazzo della Ragione** with a medieval tower, Torre del Comune—take the lift to the rooftop view over the Po valley to the Alps.

The town's most venerable edifice, on Piazza del Duomo, is the 12th-century Romanesque church of **Santa Maria Maggiore.** Notice the finely carved, monumental porch and slender campanile. The Baroque interior has impressive 16th-century **tapestries** and a monument to Donizetti on

Rest your feet and take in the surroundings at the Piazza Vecchia.

the west wall. The inlaid **choir stalls** and intarsia on the altar rail include designs by Lorenzo Lotto and Andreo Previtali.

Adjacent to the church is the Renaissance **Colleoni Chapel,** the *condottiere*'s extravagant mausoleum in red, white, and green marble. The lavish façade illustrating classical and Biblical allegory is no masterpiece, but it gives wonderful expression to the old soldier's legendary braggadocio (see page 61). Some of the windows' pillars reproduce the shape of cannon barrels that Colleoni pioneered on the battlefield. Inside is his tomb, a gilded wooden equestrian statue, and ceiling frescos by Tiepolo.

A short walk from the Città Alta's Porta Sant'Agostino, the **Galleria dell'Accademia Carrara** stands on the north-east side of the Lower City. It includes a *Madonna and Child* by Mantegna, and paintings by Bellini, Lotto, Raphael, Titian, Botticelli, and Carpaccio.

Among the foreign artists represented are Holbein, Rubens, Velazquez, and El Greco.

THE LAKES

Italy's most famous lakes—Maggiore, Como, and Garda—are within easy reach of Milan. A popular destination with the Italians themselves, they are at their best, and busiest, in spring, when the luxuriant vegetation is in full bloom.

Lake Maggiore

Blessed with a temperate, mild climate and luxuriant vegetation, Lake Maggiore is a watery arm curving along the foot of the Alps, 64 km (40 miles) long and nearly 5 km (3 miles) at its widest point, with the "elbow" at Baveno. With the Ticino river as its main affluent, it covers 212 sq km (82 square miles), one fifth of it being at the Locarno (northern) end, in Switzerland.

Since 1748, the west shore has been part of Piedmont, but it has never lost its identity as part of Lombardy since the domination of the Visconti in the Middle Ages and the presence of the Borromeo family from the 15th century.

The dynasty which gave Milan its greatest cardinals also gave its name to the lake's romantic islands—the Borromean Islands. These are still owned by the family, as are the lake's fishing rights.

Trains from Milan take one hour to Arona at the lake's southern end or 90 minutes to Laveno on the eastern shore.

Varese

With its own little lake nearby, this pleasant shoe-manufacturing town, 56 km (35 miles) northwest of Milan, makes a handy stop for drivers heading for the Laveno car ferry at Lake Maggiore.

The handsome public gardens (**Giardini Pubblici**) offer a great view north to the Alps, beyond the fine Baroque **Palazzo Estense** which serves as the town hall. Laid out in classically Italian style, the gardens harbour the 18th-century Villa Mirabello, home to the **Museo Civico** (municipal museum), a small museum devoted to local affairs, including antiquities unearthed from the surrounding area and some paintings by historic painters from Varese.

Borromean Islands

Close to the western shore of Lake Maggiore, the *Isole Borromee* are celebrated for their Baroque palazzi and magnificent gardens. All are within easy reach by boat from Stresa, Baveno, or Pallanza.

Isola Bella is named after Isabella, wife of Count Carlo Borromeo, who planned the island haven for her. The soil in its ten tiers of terraced gardens had to be brought by barge from the mainland.

Besides admirable works by Annibale Carracci, Tiepolo, Zuccarelli, and Giordano, the 17th-century **palazzo** is decorated with landscape paintings by Antonio Tempesta, who used the island as a refuge after being accused of murdering his wife.

Down in the basement is a wonderful collection of 18th-century puppets. The terraced gardens constitute one of the finest examples of the Italian formal style. View the lake from the uppermost terrace, by the unicorn statue that is the Borromeo family emblem.

Isola dei Pescatori (Fishermen's Island) is, indeed, simply a peaceful fishing village with tiny, narrow streets and a pleasant little restaurant.

Isola Madre, farther out in the lake, is the largest of the islands. The **botanical gardens** set around the 16th-century

The palace on Isola Bella is a grand monument to the Borromeo family, one of the richest in Italy.

palazzo here are renowned for their rhododendrons, camellias (April), and azaleas (May), as well as pheasants and raucous white peacocks all year round.

Stresa

Since the 19th century, and particularly since the construction of Napoleon's Simplon Road through the Alps, Stresa has been the lake's principal resort, boasting the most luxurious hotels. The lakeside **Lungolago promenade** is famous for its flowers and bewitching views of the islands. On the southern outskirts, in the **Villa Pallavicino** (1850), visit the beautiful, hillside botanical gardens which occupy sprawling parkland laid out in English, French, and Italian style.

You can also take the cable car up to the peak of the **Mottarone** (at a vertiginously high 1,491 metres/4,892 feet), from where there are exhilarating views of the Lombardy lakes, Alps, and Po valley. Alternatively, the toll road will get you there via the **Giardino Alpinia** (Alpine Gardens), displaying a quite staggering 2,000 varieties of mountain plants.

Verbania

Just around the "elbow" of Lake Maggiore from Stresa, this handsome resort shares, along with **Pallanza** and **Intra,** a microclimate of hot summers and gloriously mild winters that support a carefully nurtured, semi-tropical vegetation. The town takes its name from the vervain tea herb which grows here in profusion (as do magnolias).

Just north of Verbania with a direct service by boat, **Villa Taranto** offers the lake's most spectacular **botanical gardens** (from April to October). The 16 hectares (40 acres) of parkland were bequeathed to Italy in 1931 by a Scottish soldier, one Captain Neil McEacharn. Among the fountains, waterfalls, basins, and lily ponds, you will find several thousand varieties of plants. They have been brought from all over the world and gradually acclimatized here over the years. This is the only place where some Egyptian plants, known from mythology, will grow—apart from the Nile valley.

Baveno

North of Stresa, this quieter little resort was visited by Queen Victoria, who promenaded here when staying at the nearby Castello Bianco. Baveno is famous for its local red and white granite used in the construction of St. Peter's basilica in Rome. The octagonal, Renaissance **baptistery** on the main square and the 12th-century **parish church** are both worth a look.

Locarno and Ascona (Switzerland)

Don't forget your passport if you intend crossing the border into the Swiss part of the lake. (The last stop on the Italian side, Cannobio, is famous for its anti-smuggling flotilla of *torpediere* boats.) Locarno is one of the few places in the Alpine country where you can see subtropical foliage such as banana plants, date palms, and orange trees.

Milan's lords were once on these shores, as is testified by the handsome remains of the **Castello Visconti.** Its 15th-century courtyard, surrounded by graceful arcades, leads to the **Museo Civico,** which harbours a rich archaeological collection including many Roman relics.

A few streets away is the airy, curving **Piazza Grande,** the city's main square. Its arcades shelter Locarno's annual International Film Festival, at which films are shown on an outdoor screen.

Uphill from the Piazza is the **Città Vecchia,** the old town of stately villas, time-worn apartment buildings, hidden gardens, and venerable churches. Among the turreted mansions, look out for **Casa Rusca** in Piazza Sant'Antonio, containing the art collection donated by French-born sculptor Jean Arp, a founder of the Dada movement and leading surrealist. He died here in 1966.

A five-minute funicular ride from the centre of town leads to the sanctuary of **Madonna del Sasso,** perched on its steep rock. For centuries, pilgrims have made the trip on foot to pray at the site of a miraculous vision in the church. From the church, you can take a cable car and then a chair-lift to the **Cimetta** belvedere, giving a superb panorama of both town and lake.

Ascona is separated from Locarno by the Maggia river flowing into the lake. Once a simple fishing village, it has become popular with artists and writers. Favoured in the past by dancer Isadora Duncan, painter Paul Klee, and the exiled Lenin, it now hosts frequent art exhibitions and an annual festival of classical music. The **lake promenade** has lively outdoor cafés and restaurants, and the side streets are occupied by Swiss jewellery shops and Italian fashion boutiques.

Lake Como

Embraced by green wooded escarpments, the lake favoured by some of England's most romantic 19th-century poets—Wordsworth, Shelley, and Byron—retains a certain wistful atmosphere for the leisure hours of the Milanese and lovers from the north.

Its three elongated arms meet at the promontory of its principal resort, Bellagio. The main river feeding the lake is the Adda, flowing in from the north and through the southeast arm at Lecco, last stronghold of Como's old-fashioned *lucie* fishing boats. Trains from Milan to the town of Como take one hour.

An aerial view of Lago di Como, arguably one of the world's most romantic bodies of water.

Como

This silk-factory town (population 100,000) lies 49 km (30 miles) up the A9 *autostrada* from Milan. The *centro storico* retains the chequerboard plan of the ancient Roman town of Comum. Famous for its library and schools, Como was the home of writers Pliny the Elder—who died while observing the volcanic eruption of Mt. Vesuvius that engulfed Pompeii on 24 August A.D. 79—and his nephew and adopted son, Pliny the Younger (A.D. 62–120).

Como's other famous son, 18th-century electricity pioneer Alessandro Volta, is honoured with a monument in the lake-front **Giardini Pubblici** (Public Gardens). The Neo-classical **Tempio Volta** displays the scientific instruments with which he developed the "volt" as a unit of electrical measurement.

The **Lungo Lario** lakefront promenade is the natural setting for the town's *passeggiata* in the late afternoon, past the cruise-boats' landing stage, and the hotels, cafés, and restaurants on the **Piazza Cavour,** social meeting-place *par excellence*.

The town's handsome, Gothic-Renaissance **cathedral** (fifth century) is crowned by a superb Baroque dome added in 1744 by Turin's great architect, Filippo Juvarra. On the façade, both Plinys Elder and Younger are portrayed in seated sculptures on either side of the central doorway. In the lofty Gothic interior, notice the 16th-century **tapestries** in the nave and, in the south (right) aisle chapels, altar paintings by Bernardino Luini. Next to the cathedral is the arcaded 13th-century **Broletto** (town hall) in white, grey, and red marble.

Bellagio

This tranquil resort juts out into the lake on a hilly promontory. Up on the heights above the town, the elegant 18th-century **Villa Serbelloni** (not to be confused with the Ville Serbelloni luxury hotel down near the lakefront) stands in the middle of a beautiful park of rose trees, camellias, magnolias, and pomegranates. At the southern end of town, the **lido** offers a bracing swim.

Lake cruises—and the car ferry—leave from the Lungolario Marconi. When looking for gifts, remember

Dense greenery covers the hills surrounding Lake Como.

Como's fifth-century Gothic-Renaissance cathedral holds prized tapestries, and altar paintings by Bernadino Luini.

that Bellagio craftsmen are renowned for their silk weaving and olive-wood carving.

Excursions around Lake Como

Lake Como's most attractive stretch of water is its southwest arm. If you're based at Bellagio, the only way to see the colourful grottoes and misty waterfall at **Nesso** is by taking a boat cruise south from Lezzeno. The western shore of the lake is lined with villas that are nestled in fragrant gardens.

At **Cernobbio,** just north of Como, the 16th-century Villa d'Este is now a grand hotel (see page 135) where you can take tea and stroll among the cypresses and magnolias.

Between the genteel resort towns of **Tremezzo** and **Cadenabbia,** you'll find one of the lake's most beautiful residences (open to the public), the 18th-century **Villa Carlotta.** There's a marvellous view of the lake from its terraced gardens, which are famous for their display of camellias, azaleas, and rhododendrons in late April and May.

Lake Garda

Surrounded by rolling green hills, Lake Garda is graced with vineyards (notably those of Bardolino), lemon trees, olives, and noble cedars. People seeking a restful holiday enjoy its mild winters and mellow summers, and Garda has long been popular with visitors from Austria, Switzerland, and Germany.

On the west shore, the people of Salò, where Gasparo Bertolotti is said to have designed the violin, suggest his inspiration came from the contours of the lake. Italy's largest lake is shaped less like a violin than a banjo, however, measuring 52 km (32 miles) from the cliffs at the tip of its neck down to the base of the broad "sound box." At its widest, it is 18 km (11 miles); its surface is 370 square km (143 square miles).

Gabriele d'Annunzio (1863–1938)

Many Italians will tell you that Gabriele d'Annunzio was the country's best and worst poet of the 20th century. An outrageous provocateur and an insatiable lover of ladies and boys, he made Salvador Dali look like an insurance salesman.

His reputation as a frenzied champion of Italian nationalism soared in August 1918 when he led a squadron of ten planes across the Austrian border to drop leaflets proclaiming: "We could have dropped bombs on you, but we send you our three-coloured salute, the three colours of freedom." He "liberated" Rijeka (Fiume) from the Croats in 1919 at the head of a platoon of black-shirted soldiers, thereby inventing the Fascist uniform for Mussolini, with whom he became close friends. Decorating his home with reproductions of the Sistine Chapel ceiling and Christian martyrs, this most pagan of Catholics stated: "St. Francis was the first Fascist and I the last Franciscan."

The town of Brescia is the most convenient of the large towns on the way to Garda, with rail and *autostrada* links to the resort town of Desenzano del Garda, some 118 km (73 miles) from Milan.

Brescia

Famous for weapons manufacturing (notably Biretta guns), Brescia suffered as an obvious target in World War II, but has rebounded as an ebullient modern city (population 429,000) with an attractive *centro storico*. Just half an hour from Lake Garda, it has preserved and restored the historic core around the **Piazza del Duomo.**

The most interesting of the two churches here is not the present cathedral—a rather ponderous, 17th-century affair —but its Romanesque predecessor, the large, brick Duomo

Rocca Scaligera, the castle at Sirmione, was built right out into the water.

Vecchio, usually known as the **Rotonda.** Inside this round, 12th-century building are a series of notable paintings by Moretto da Brescia, including *The Assumption* over the high altar and, in the choir, *St. Luke, St. Mark, Elijah Asleep,* and the *Sacrifice of Isaac*.

The delightful **Piazza della Loggia** is valiantly resisting the brutal modern office blocks that tower above the neighbouring Piazza della Vittoria.

At the western end of the square is the handsome 16th-century **town hall** (*Loggia*), graced with an early Renaissance pawnshop, **Monte di Pietà,** on the south side.

The art collection of the **Pinacoteca Tosio-Martinengo** (Via Martinengo da Barco) is devoted principally to Brescia's own Renaissance masters—Moretto, Vicenzo Foppa, Romanino, and Moroni—but also has fine works by Renaissance masters Raphael, Lotto, and Tintoretto.

Desenzano del Garda

This lively resort is the gateway to Lake Garda. Plan your itinerary at a café in the attractive, arcaded **Piazza Capelletti** on the lakefront, or simply watch the world go by.

The nearby parish church of **Santa Maria Maddelena** has a *Last Supper* by Tiepolo in its Chapel of the Sacrament, while in the Via degli Scavi are the ruins of a **Roman villa.**

Sirmione

Perched on a narrow promontory, the fishing village and renowned spa and resort of Sirmione offers a unique view of the lake. At the tip of the promontory in a romantic setting of olive trees are the **Grotte di Catullo,** in fact the vaulted ruins of a Roman villa. They are somewhat hopefully attributed to the poet Catullus, who had his summer residence at Sirmione in the first century B.C. Fresco fragments from the same period can be seen in the site's remarkable **Antiquarium.**

One of the best vantage points is the tower of the 13th-century castle, **Rocca Scaligera.** It was built out onto the water beside the town gate by the Scaligeri lords of Verona.

Sirmione's *Stazione Termale* (spa) on the northern edge of town is there to help restore tired bones and muscles, skin problems, and breathing, from March to November.

The Boiola sulphur springs, famous since ancient Roman times, rise from the lake bed just north of the peninsula at a temperature of 69°C (156°F).

Gardesana Occidentale (West Shore)

The drive along the winding road cut through the cliffs of the lake's west shore is one of the most spectacular in Italy.

The pretty resort town of **Salò** is set in a narrow bay. With its historical museum housed in the 16th-century Palazzo della Magnifica Patria, it tries to live down its unhappy moment as the capital of Mussolini's puppet republic, installed by the Germans in the month of September 1943.

☛ **Gardone Riviera** is a fashionable resort much appreciated for its parks and botanical gardens, and as base for hikes up and around **Monte Lavino.**

Above the town, in Gardone di Sopra, is a 20th-century "folly," **Il Vittoriale,** the bizarre and disturbing residence of Gabriele d'Annunzio, poet, adventurer, and Fascist (see page 73). Melancholy gardens of dense shrubbery, dark laurel, and parades of cypresses lead past a Greek theatre to a mausoleum with the writer's green marble sarcophagus flanked by those of his disciples. It overlooks the prow of a World War I warship, the *Puglia*, which was hauled up the hillside as the *pièce de résistance* of this macabre villa-museum.

The villa houses two cars in which d'Annunzio drove himself to the World War I battlefront and the aircraft from which he dropped his propaganda leaflets over Vienna. His library includes a collection of precious 16th-century books, rare manuscripts, and also an Austrian machine gun.

Gardesana Orientale (East Shore)

The southeastern corner of lake Garda, which belongs to the province of Verona, can be visited on a boat trip. First port of call from Sirmione is the resort town of **Peschiera,** which has retained old ramparts from its late days as a stronghold of the Venetian empire. **Bardolino,** which is famous for its lusty red wines, boasts the remains of a Scaliger castle and also two picturesque medieval churches, the ninth-century San Zeno and 12th-century San Severo.

The Vittoriale did not crash into the hillside—she was hoisted here by Gabriele d'Annunzio.

The town of **Garda** has a charming promenade, while 3 km (2 miles) farther west is the cypress-lined headland of **Punta San Vigilio.** From here, in the Villa Guarnienti's Italian-style gardens, you can immerse yourself in one of the lake's most enchanting views.

WHAT TO DO

There's lots to do other than sightseeing in and around Milan and the lakes. We offer some suggestions here for shopping, entertainment, sports, and what to do with the kids.

SHOPPING

There's plenty to buy in Milan and the lake resorts, but don't expect to find any bargains. The Milanese know the value of their design sense and put a more-than-appropriate price on it. One intriguing comeback due to the economic crisis of the 1990s is the ancient art of haggling—although it's much more subtle nowadays. Make a discreet enquiry about a possible *sconto* (discount), and you may get a pleasant surprise.

Flea Markets

The most popular takes place along the **Naviglio Grande** on the Via Ripa Porta Ticinese on the last Sunday of each month. It starts at dawn—the best time to get there—and tends to close mid-afternoon. Find your bargain and have your first *caffè* or *cappuccino* of the day at a canal-bank café.

More chic (and expensive) is the **Brera** neighbourhood market on the third Saturday of each month at Via Fiori Chiari, Via Madonnina, and Piazza Formentini. It starts at the more respectable hour of 10:00 A.M. but goes on almost until midnight. Outside Milan, **Bergamo** (see page 62) holds a flea market in the Upper City's Piazza Vecchia on the third Sunday of the month.

What to Buy

Antiques: The "Montenapo" district (see page 36) is the heart of the antiques-dealers' territory. Try the following: Canelli at

Calendar of Events

Details of trade and fashion shows in Milan (Metro: Amendola Fiera) are available from Ente Autonomo Fiera Internazionale di Milano, Largo Domodossola 1, 20145 Milano; tel. (02) 49971, fax (02) 49977179.

January: Milan. 6 January, *Befana* Epiphany (Twelfth Night) procession between Sant'Ambrogio and Sant'Eustorgio.

February: Sei Giorno di Ciclismo (Six Days of Cycling) at forum di Assago. Call (02) 488571 for details.

February/March: Milan. Mardi Gras Carnival street parade and parties (Thursday, Saturday, and Tuesday before Lent).

March: Milan. 18-22 March, *Cinque Giornate* celebrations recall the 1848 uprising against Austria, around Porta Vittoria. Also in Milan: International Contemporary Art Fair and *Milano Collezioni*, women's autumn/winter collections.

April: Milan. *Fiera d'Aprile*, major international trade fair.

May: Legnano. May 29, Medieval-costumed battle pageant commemorating the 1176 Lombard victory (see page 17).

May-June: Bergamo. International piano festival.

June: Milan. Navigli canal district festival. Comacina. Fireworks over Lake Como for midsummer Island Feast of *San Giovanni*.

July: Milan. *Milano Collezioni Uomo* menswear collections.

August: Milan. *Vacanze a Milano* festival in Parco Sempione. Gardone. Sailing regatta on Lake Garda.

August-September: Stresa. *Settimane Musicale*, music festival in churches and on Isola Bella.

September: Monza. Grand Prix Formula I motor racing. Como. *Autunna Musicale* international music festival (until November).

October: Milan. *Milano Collezioni* women's spring/summer designer collections.

November: Everywhere. November 1, All Saints' Day, remembrance with flowers and cakes: *pane dei morti* ("bread for the dead").

December: Milan. Christmas Market on Piazza del Duomo. On 24 December: Laveno. Underwater crib on Lake Maggiore.

Milanese metalware is made in an unrivalled range of innovative styles.

14 Via Santo Spirito for Italian **Baroque furniture;** on 22 Via Spiga, visit Subert for **scientific instruments;** and, at 46 Via Spiga, Brucoli offers a selection of beautiful antique **jewellery.**

Clothes: Milan is Italy's undisputed fashion capital and the centuries-old Italian sense of line and colour quite often outshines Paris, New York, and Tokyo. Designer clothes may be cheaper back home, but you will find a much greater selection here and, of course, the latest styles are shown in Milanese stores prior to shipment overseas. For both women's and men's clothes, the master couturiers — Versace, Armani, Moschino, Missoni, Fendi, Ermenegildo Zegna, Krizia, Gianfranco Ferré — all have their boutiques on and around the famous "Montenapo," principally along Via Monte Napoleone itself, Via della Spiga, and Via Sant'Andrea.

For the best in Italian **shoes,** try Cesare Paciotti, Ferragamo, and Fratelli Rossetti; for underwear, more aptly known as **lingerie,** Pratesi; for exclusive **beachwear,** Cavallini; for the softest, most exquisite **leather,** Gucci, Bottega Veneto and Nazareno Gabrielli. (Like fashion itself, boutique addresses can change rapidly. However, the "Montenapo" neighbourhood is small and cosy enough to find each designer without much trouble.)

Craftwork: The quality of traditional craftmanship outside Milan can still be admired in the ornaments and utensils of wrought iron, turned wood, and embossed copper at the pretty city of Bergamo. Lake Maggiore resorts are especially known for Arona ceramics, Como and Bellagio for silk and carved olive wood, and Brescia for hunting rifles.

Gourmet Foods: In Milan, the great gift speciality is the mountainous, gargantuan *panettone* brioche with raisins. For cheeses from all over Italy, visit Peck—Casa del Formaggio, Via Speronari 3 (Metro: Duomo). In Milan's speciality food shops you'll also find the finest varieties of olive oil and other delicacies. Lake Garda resorts are also justly famous for their olive oil and the price is often better there than in Milan.

Household Accessories: Milan has an unrivalled range of innovative styles in everything from fountain pens and lamps to kitchenware, espresso machines, and other household

Simply window-shopping on the pedestrian-friendly streets of Milan is a pleasure.

gadgets. The area to search is on and around Via Monte Napoleone, Corso Matteoti, and Corso Monforto.

Jewellery: The country's top jewellers share the "Montenapo" district with the fashion designers. The leading shops are: Bulgari, Buccellati, Calderoni, Jacente, and Dal Vecchio (for antique jewels).

Lake Garda's goldsmiths are highly respected, with boutiques at all the major resorts, and Brescia is known for its fine silverware. For upmarket designer watches, it's worth taking a cruise on Lake Maggiore across the Swiss border to Locarno, where you'll find the greatest choice.

Modern Furniture: Even if you're not contemplating carrying an armchair home, it can be interesting to do some astute window shopping here to help place early orders with distributors back where you live. The major stores are conveniently grouped along Via Manzoni.

The showrooms of the revered *Domus* magazine, at number 37, are a barometer of avant-garde and Classical modern tastes in home design. Other important outlets are Poltrona

Local vendors display their wares in street-stalls at Isola dei Pescatori.

Frau (number 20) and Post-Design Memphis (number 27 via Mosconi).

Toys: Long before Geppetto made Pinocchio, Italian toys, especially puppets, had their very own special magic. For the delight of children, try a few of the best Milan shops, namely: Cagnoni, Corso Vercelli 38 (Metro: Conciliazione); Giocattoli e Giochi, Città del Sole, Via Orefici 5 (Metro: Cairoli); and Tiys Center, Via Mauro Macchi 29 (near Stazione Centrale).

ENTERTAINMENT

Pride of place—if you can get a seat—must go to the **opera** at La Scala (see page 35), which opens its annual season with a gala première on St. Ambrose's feast day, on December 7. It is still one of the best opera houses in the world, as well as one of the most prestigious in the eyes of the singers and conductors. Unfortunately for those visiting Milan before the year 2001, La Scala will be closed for renovation until that time. Smaller but equally exquisite productions are staged at the Teatro Lirico, Via Larga 14, where tickets may be more easily obtained.

Concerts of **classical music** are also much in demand, notably at the Piccola Scala (near the main La Scala) on Via Filodrammatici, and at Teatro Manzoni on Via Manzoni. The RAI (National Italian Radio) symphony orchestra and the Quartetto Italiano play regularly at the Conservatorio, Via Conservatorio 12. **Ballet** is staged at the Teatro Nazionale, Piazza Piemonte 12.

Open-air concerts are regularly held in summer in Milan, at the Castello Sforzesco's Piazza d'Armi, as well as in the lake resorts. Bergamo's enchanting Teatro Donizetti is the venue for fine opera, ballet, and classical music.

Even if your Italian is not up to much, for **theatre** try to see a production at the world famous Piccolo Teatro di Milano, Via Rivello 2, created by the great Giorgio Strehler. The troupe's communicative style transcends any language problems.

Where the Fat Lady Sings

Italy's Austrian rulers came in for a lot of criticism, but it was their taste for opera that fostered the glory of La Scala. In fact, the Italian composer Antonio Salieri, whose *Europa Riconosciuta* inaugurated the opera house in 1778, was the Habsburg court musician. By 1839, however, Giuseppe Verdi, who premièred eight of his operas at La Scala, had made it a symbol of Italy's national identity. It was only in 1898 that director Arturo Toscanini opened the repertoire to non-Italian composers with Wagner's *Meistersinger*, followed by works by Tchaikovsky, Weber, and Debussy. In 1948, Toscanini was back to reopen the opera house, restored from its wartime bombing.

The spectacular gala which opens the annual season is on the sacrosanct 7 December, feast day of the city's patron saint and Church Father, St. Ambrose. From that night onwards, until the season ends in mid-July, La Scala is still the hottest opera ticket in Europe. Most of the best tickets are in the firm hands of the old Milan gentry, who bequeath their subscription with the family jewels from generation to generation. It is nonetheless possible to get tickets—on the open or black market, through your hotel or travel agency, or you can call La Scala directly at (02) 860787 (non-residents) or (02) 860775 (residents). Tickets are limited to 2 per person. Prices vary from a few thousand lire up to L150,000–200,000. The best seats are in the Orchestra rows C–O and the cheaper but excellent front row of the first balcony. La Scala is closing for a complete renovation from 1998–2001.

No singer's career is complete without a performance at La Scala opera house.

On the west side of town, the Palalido and Palazzetto dello Sport stage big **jazz** and **rock music** concerts. Palatrussardi, on Via S. Elia, also stages major musical events.

You can enjoy music in a more intimate setting, over a drink, at the bars in the Navigli quarters, the most popular being the Scimmie at Via Ascanio Sforza 49. The Ca'Bianca and Capolinea, both on Via Ludovico il Moro, also enjoy a good reputation.

In the smarter Brera quarter, try a visit to the more sedate Club 2 on Via Formentini or the popular student hangout, Il Giamaica, Via Brera 32. These areas have several **discos,** which are an excellent choice for a night out as well.

SPORTS

As in almost all Italian cities, soccer is king, but there are plenty of other sporting activities on offer as well. For more detailed information about access to Milan's sporting facilities, contact the CMSR (Centro Milanese per lo Sport e la Ricreazione, Piazza Diaz 1A (tel. 02-801466). Alternatively, consult the city's main tourist information office on Piazza del Duomo (see page 127).

Many of the resort hotels at the lakes have their own tennis and swimming facilities. Enquire at the local tourist office (see page 126).

Tennis and Golf: The most easily accessible tennis courts (covered and open, hard, and clay) from the city centre are those at the Lido di Milano, Piazzale Lotto 15 (Metro Lotto). Golf Club Milano's 9- and 18-hole courses are located in Monza's Villa Reale Park, entrance at Porta San Giorgio (tel. 039-303081), but check first with the Milan tourist information office about temporary club membership. (The

Vroom-Vroom!

When eight snappy little Fiat 804s inaugurated the 5.8-km- (3½-mile) long Monza Grand Prix circuit on September 10, 1922, they averaged 140 km/h (85 mph) over 80 laps. These days, the Williams-Renaults and others have pushed the average up well over 215 km/h (135 mph).

The legendary Juan Fangio notched up his first victory at Monza in 1950 in an Alfa Romeo. Ferrari had to wait until 1960 for its victory, with American driver Phil Hill.

Grandstand seats for the September Grand Prix are difficult to obtain. A full programme is available from the Autodromo Nazionale di Monza; tel. (039) 248212.

Tennis at the Monza park is a great way to take advantage of a bright afternoon.

Monza park also has tennis courts and facilities for swimming, grass-hockey, and polo.)

Baseball and Basketball: Appropriate to its name, the Presidente Kennedy sports centre, Via Olivieri 15 (tel. 02-47996783), has a very respectable baseball diamond, while the Lida di Milano, Piazzale Lotto 15, boasts a good basketball court.

Swimming and Watersports: The Lido di Milano, Piazzale Lotto 15 (Metro Lotto) has a heated indoor pool (as well as a **gymnasium** for a pre-swimming workout). A little further out at the Parco Forlanini on the east side of town, the Saini sports centre, Via Corelli 136, has both the above plus an open-air pool.

Swimming in the lakes can be a very bracing affair, but the major resorts do offer amenities for **water-skiing, windsurfing,** and **sailing.** For details of **fishing** in the lakes, enquire at local tourist information offices.

The many lakes in the area around Milan offer rich fishing opportunities.

Spectator Sports: There can be few more exciting sporting spectacles in Europe than a **football** (soccer) match out at the Meazza Stadium (San Siro), Via Piccolomini 5. The city's two teams, AC and Inter Milan, are among the finest in the world. All their games involve high drama but when the two teams play against each other, the composition is worthy of Giuseppe Verdi.

There is also **horse-racing** to watch at the San Siro and at Monza's Mirabello race courses, while **ice-hockey** matches take place at the Palazzo del Ghiaccio, Via Piranesi 14 (Stazione Porta Vittoria).

Motor rallies are held during the summer months around Bergamo, Brescia, and Como. The region's biggest sporting event remains the **Grand Prix** Formula 1 motor race at Monza in September (see page 86).

MILAN WITH CHILDREN

The secret to keeping children amused in Milan is to make the most of the city's sights, even if they're not geared specifically towards youngsters. At the **Duomo,** for instance, a visit to the cathedral roof is always a great success. Also popular are Leonardo da Vinci's inventions at the **Science**

Museum (see page 43). Taking to the water is usually a successful ploy: in Milan itself there are **canal cruises** on the Navigli, while at the lakes there are countless boat trips up and down the shores. The lakes also offer **botanical gardens.** They may enjoy **skating** at the Palaghiaccio in Via Piranesi.

Parks: Milan has two very fine parks close to the city centre. Behind the Castello Sforzesco, **Parco Sempione** (Metro Lanza) provides plenty of space for the kids to let off steam—or to have a picnic with the family. Besides its tropical fish, the **aquarium** (Via Gadio 2) has a wonderful collection of creepy, crawly reptiles. In August, the park hosts a summer festival, *Vacanze a Milano* (Holidays in Milan), offering free theatre and musical shows, dancing, and open-air restaurants.

In the **Giardini Pubblici** (Metro: Palestro), you will find duck ponds, pony-rides, dodgem cars, and a miniature train. There is also a **Planetarium** here and dinosaurs in the **Natural History Museum.**

Puppets: Not far from the Science Museum is the Teatro delle Marionette, a delightful, privately run puppet theatre at Via Olivetani 3B, tel. 469-4440 (Metro: Conciliazione). When visiting the Borromean Islands on Lake Maggiore (see page 65), visit the 18th-century puppets in the palazzo on Isola Bella. You can always head for Milan's toy shops (see page 83).

Special Events: Every Saturday morning, **stamp** and **coin collectors** gather to exchange treasures on the Piazza degli Affari by the *Borso* (Stock Exchange, Metro: Cordusio). You will find bargain buys within pocket-money range. A **bird and goldfish** market is held on Sunday morning in front of the Palazzo Reale, from March to June and from September to November.

In April, kids may want to take their dads to the **Monza Motorcycle Grand Prix**. Call the Monza Autodromo (tel. 039-2482212) for more information on dates and times. A May highlight is the live **chess game** in medieval costume in the Greco neighbourhood.

For other annual festive occasions, see the Calendar of Events on page 79; exact dates and other details are available from Tourist Information (see page 126), APT, Via Marconi 1 (tel. 02-725241).

It's not hard to find diversions for young travellers at Parco Sempione.

EATING OUT

It is the opinion of many a stout gourmand and not a few slimmer gourmets, too, that Italian cooking is the most enjoyable in the world. Milanese cuisine is very highly rated by the Italians themselves. It's tasty and for the most part simple (though not without its refinements), colourful, and always sheer good fun to eat, whether it's a steaming plate of pasta or the famous local veal stew of *osso buco*.

WHERE TO EAT

Male waiters are called *cameriere* (kamayreeairay), female *cameriera* (kahmayreeairah)

Only in a few hotels catering specifically for foreign tourists will you find an English- or American-style **breakfast.** On all other occasions, head for a good *caffè* on the piazza and settle, quite happily, for the local *prima colazione* of superb coffee, *espresso* black, or *cappucino* with foaming hot milk (served sprinkled with powdered chocolate in the best establishments), and a sweet roll or toast. Italian tea tends to be fairly anaemic, but the hot chocolate is excellent.

An ideal option for those adopting a healthy "sightseer's diet" of one main meal a day, with just a snack for **lunch,** are stand-up bars known as *tavola calda* which serve sandwiches and hot or cold dishes at the counter. If you want to picnic in the park or out in the country, get your sandwiches made up for you at the *pizzicheria* delicatessen. Ask for *panino ripieno*, a bread roll filled with whatever sausage, cheese, or salad you choose from the display at the counter.

For **dinner,** even if you're not overly budget conscious, bear in mind that, often, the most elaborate restaurant (*ristorante*), where prices match the opulence of the décor, is rarely the best value. In a family-run *trattoria* or even a Neapolitan-style *pizzeria*—which will serve much more than simply pizza—both the ambience and the food are infinitely more enjoyable and have more real character.

For more details, see the list of Recommended Restaurants starting on page 137. Remember, it's the custom to round off the bill with an extra tip in addition to the service charge.

WHAT TO EAT

Besides offering their own local specialities, Lombardy and Milan restaurants do serve the classical cuisine of their honoured rivals in Tuscany, Bologna, and Naples. Despite the plethora of sauces that accompany pasta, the essence of Italian cooking is in its simplicity: freshwater fish from the lakes cooked with, say, just a touch of fennel; other seafood (usually brought in from the Ligurian coast) served "straight," cold, as an hors d'œuvre; or a juicy charcoal-grilled Florentine steak with vegetables.

Fresh fruit from the local street stand is a light alternative to a full Italian meal.

Antipasti

Any decent *trattoria* sets out on a long table near the entrance a truly artistic display of its *antipasti* (hors d'œuvre). Get to know the delicacies on offer by making up your own assortment (**antipasto misto**). Both attractive and tasty are cold *peperoni*—green, yellow, and red peppers grilled, skinned, and marinated in olive oil and a little lemon juice. Mushrooms (*funghi*), baby marrows (*zucchini*), aubergines (*melanzane*), artichokes (*carciofi*), and sliced fennel (*finocchio*) are also served cold, with a tangy dressing (*pinzimonio*). One of the most refreshing hors d'œuvre is *mozzarella alla caprese*, slices of soft buffalo cheese and tomato sprinkled with basil, olive oil, and pepper.

Try tuna fish (*tonno*) with white beans and onions (*fagioli e cipolle*). Mixed seafood hors d'œuvre (**antipasto di mare**) may include any of the following: scampi, prawns (*gamberi*), mussels (*cozze*), fresh sardines (*sarde*), and chewy but delicious squid (*calamari*) and octopus (*polpi*).

Paper-thin ham from Parma or San Daniele is served with melon (*prosciutto con melone*) or, even better, fresh figs (*con fichi*). Most **salami** is mass-produced in Milan factories, but some local restaurants do "import" farm-produced sausage from Bologna, Florence, Genoa, or Ferrara.

The most popular **soups** are mixed vegetable (*minestrone*) and clear soup (*brodo*), either plain or with an egg beaten in (*stracciatella*). Brescia is famous for its soups with ravioli or rice, the latter much more savoury than its name—*minestra sporca* or "dirty soup."

Pasta

Despite our diet-conscious era, Italian restaurants traditionally serve **pasta** as an introductory course and not as the main dish. While they won't say anything, even the friendliest restaurant owners might raise a sad eyebrow if you make a whole meal out of a plate of spaghetti. It is said that there are as many different forms of Italian pasta noodles as there are French cheese—some 360 at last count, with new forms being created every year. Each sauce—tomato, cheese, cream, meat, or fish—needs its own kind of noodle. In this land of artists, the pasta's shape and texture form an essential part of the taste, and pasta manufacturers commission top architects to design new noodle configurations.

Besides spaghetti and macaroni, the worldwide popularity of pasta has familiarized us with *tagliatelle* (ribbon noodles), baked *lasagne* (layers of pasta laced with a meat and béchamel sauce), rolled *canelloni*, and stuffed *ravioli*. From there, you launch into the lusty poetry of *tortellini* and *cappelletti* (variations on ravioli), or elliptically curved *linguine*, flat *pappardelle*, quill-shaped *penne*, and the corrugated *rigatoni*. Discover the other 350 shapes for yourself.

Following the pasta profusion, there are almost as many **sauces.** A subtle variation on the ubiquitous *bolognese* meat sauce is made with chopped chicken livers, white wine, and celery. Others range from the simplest and spiciest *aglio e olio* (just garlic, olive oil, and chilli peppers), *marinara* (tomato), *carbonara* (chopped bacon and eggs), *pesto* (basil and garlic ground up in olive oil with pine nuts and Parmesan cheese), and *vongole* (tomato and clams), to the succulent *lepre* (hare in red wine) and startling but wonderful *al nero*—pasta blackened by the ink of the cuttlefish. Parmesan is not automatically added to every pasta dish: don't be ashamed to ask for it.

Risotto

For Lombardy's princes and peasants alike, the Po valley paddies have made this grand rice dish a worthy rival to pasta. Connoisseurs argue the relative merits of the Milan and Bergamo recipes. The rice has to be round and creamy, never long and dry. It's cooked slowly in white wine, beef marrow, butter (not oil), and saffron, with Parmesan cheese melted in at the end of the cooking for the proper smooth finish. The result is especially delicious when blended with seafood, chicken, or mushrooms.

Main Dish

Of the **meats,** veal (*vitello*) takes pride of place. If you try the veal cutlet (*cotoletta alla Milanese*, pan-fried in bread-crumbs—a Milanese speciality), the locals will be upset if you suggest this is a relic of the Habsburg empire and a descendent of the *Wiener Schnitzel*. You're on diplomatically safer ground with the delicious all-Italian *osso buco* (stewed veal shinbone) or *scaloppine* (veal fillets with lemon)—or then again the *vitello tonnato* (veal in tuna fish sauce) or *alla fiorentina* (spinach sauce).

Consider dining al fresco for a relaxing and romantic Milanese evening.

It may be shaped like a melon, but provolone is a cheese made from buffalo milk.

The ever popular *saltimbocca* ("jump in the mouth") is an originally Roman veal roll with ham, sage, and Marsala. Calf's liver (*fegato*) is served *alla milanese* in breadcrumbs. Alternatively, it can be served *alla veneziana*, thinly sliced and sauteéd with onions in olive oil.

Beef (*manzo*), lamb (*agnello*), pork (*maiale*), and chicken (*pollo*) are most often grilled or roasted (*al forno*). People with robust stomachs might like to tackle Milanese *busecca*, tripe with white beans, or *casoeula*, pork and sausages stewed in cabbage.

Fish, often displayed at a glass counter with the *antipasti*, is prepared simply—either grilled, steamed, or fried. Try the *spigola* (sea bass), *coda di rospa* (angler fish), *triglia* (red mullet), or even *pesce spada* (swordfish). Be careful when ordering the *fritto misto.* It does usually mean a mixed fry of fish, but can also be a mixed fry of breaded chicken breasts, calf's liver, veal, and vegetables. You have been warned!

***Zuppa inglese* is not an English soup but a kind of trifle, a sponge cake steeped in rum.**

Cheeses and Dessert

The famous Parmesan (*parmigiano*), far better fresh than the exported product, is eaten by itself, not just grated over soup or pasta. Try, too, the creamy Piedmontese *fontina*, Lombardy blue *gorgonzola*, tangy *provolone* buffalo cheese, as well as *taleggio* from cow's milk or *pecorino* from ewe's milk.

Nothing varies more in quality than the Italian trifle **zuppa inglese** (literally "English soup"). It may indeed be a thick but sumptuous soup of fruit, cream, cake, and Marsala, or it could just be a disappointing sweet and gooey slice of cake.

The traditional coffee trifle or **tirami sù** (literally, "pull me up") also ranges from the sublime to the sickly. **Zabaglione,** with whipped egg yolks, sugar, and Marsala, should be served warm or sent back.

Easier on the stomach is the local **fruit:** grapes (*uva*), apricots (*albicocche*), and peaches (*pesche*), not forgetting wonderful fresh figs (*fichi*), either black or green.

Ice-cream comes in a wide variety of flavours and is generally much better in an ice-cream parlour (*gelateria*) than in the restaurant.

WINES

The red wines from Lake Garda's east shores are popular but quite modest, including the light **Bardolino** and more velvety **Valpolicella.** The Milanese themselves prefer looking west to Piedmont's splendid, full-bodied **Barolo** or the fragrant **Barbera,** with an occasional sparkle that horrifies the French.

The best **Chianti Classico,** distinguished by the proud *gallo nero* (black cockerel) label stamped on the bottle, is a strong, full-bodied red with a fine bouquet. Whereas most Italian wines can—and indeed should—be drunk young, Chianti Classico ages well. A superb Tuscan rival is the earthy **Montepulciano.**

The best of Tuscany's white wines are the dry **Montecarlo** and **Vernaccia.** In Umbria, the **Orvieto** is superb, both dry and semi-dry. The light **Frascati** comes from the hills east of Rome, while from south of Turin comes the sparkling **Asti Spumante.**

For something stronger after dinner, try the anis-flavoured **sambuca** or a **grappa** brandy.

To Help You Order ...

What do you recommend?		**Cosa consiglia?**	
Do you have a set menu?		**Avete un menù a prezzo fisso?**	
I'd like a/an/some...		**Vorrei...**	
beer	**una birra**	pepper	**del pepe**
bread	**del pane**	potatoes	**delle patate**
butter	**del burro**	salad	**dell'insalata**
coffee	**un caffè**	salt	**del sale**
fish	**del pesce**	soup	**una minestra**
fruit	**della frutta**	sugar	**dello zucchero**
ice cream	**un gelato**	tea	**un tè**
meat	**del carne**	water	**dell'acqua**
wine	**del vino**	milk	**del latte**

... and Read the Menu

aglio	garlic	**formaggio**	cheese
agnello	lamb	**gamberi**	scampi, prawns
aragosta	spiny lobster	**mela**	apple
arancia	orange	**ostrica**	oyster
bistecca	beef steak	**pancetta**	bacon
brodetto	fish soup	**peperoni**	peppers
bue/manzo	beef	**pesca**	peach
carciofi	artichokes	**pesce**	fish
cipolle	onions	**piselli**	peas
coniglio	rabbit	**pollo**	chicken
costoletta	cutlet	**pomodoro**	tomato
cozze	mussels	**rognoni**	kidneys
crostacei	shellfish	**sogliola**	sole
fagioli	beans	**uova**	eggs
fegato	liver	**uva**	grapes
fichi	figs	**vitello**	veal

INDEX

HANDY TRAVEL TIPS

An A–Z Summary of Practical Information

A

ACCOMMODATION

(See also CAMPING, YOUTH HOSTELS, and the list of RECOMMENDED HOTELS starting on page 129)

Hotels, called *hotel or albergo*, are classified by the tourist authorities in categories ranging from five stars (luxury) down to one. Rates vary according to region—as well as to location, season, class, and services offered—and are fixed in agreement with the regional tourist boards in Milan and at the lakes. Being an important business city, Milan's high and low season rates for hotels are determined mainly by trade fair visitors and other commercial considerations outside the summer months, with several hotels even closing in August. At the lake resorts, where many hotels close in winter or at least after Christmas, low season is May through June and late September.

Breakfast is usually optional, and during high season at the lakes many resort hotels require guests to book a minimum of three nights half-board. Even if prices are listed as *tutto compreso* (inclusive of local taxes and service charges), check that the VAT sales tax (IVA) of 18% for five-star hotels and 9% for other categories is included.

It is advisable all year round and essential in high season to book well in advance. Reservations may be made through travel agencies or by writing directly to the hotel—in the latter case, request written confirmation. Once there, tourist offices (see page 126) can supply local hotel lists. At Milan's Linate and Malpensa airports and the Stazione Centrale, information desks provide advice and booking facilities.

Hotel reservation service: Via Palestro 24, 20124 Milan; tel. (02) 6007978, fax (02) 76003632.

Pensione. The term *pensione* covers everything from simple, family-style boarding houses to small hotels (breakfast included).

Motels are increasing and improving in service. Many have a swimming pool, tennis courts, and other sports facilities.

Self-catering. For families staying one week or more at a lake resort, a furnished apartment (*appartamento ammobiliata*) or villa is an economic and convenient alternative to a hotel. Tour operators offer self-catering packages which include travel to and from Italy. Lists of operators are available from the Italian National Tourist Office (see page 126). On the spot, check local newspaper ads or regional tourist offices for lists of companies and agents handling rentals.

Note that **Day hotels** (*albergo diurno*), situated mainly around the big railway stations, provide low-price daytime facilities—including a bathroom, hairdresser, and left-luggage—but do not provide overnight accommodation.

Do you have any vacancies?	**Avete camere libere?**
I'd like a single/double room.	**Vorrei una camera singola/doppia.**
with bath/shower/private toilet	**con bagno/doccia/gabinetto privato**
What's the price per night/week?	**Qual è il prezzo per una notte/una settimana?**

AIRPORTS *(aeroporto)*

Milan has two airports, **Malpensa,** 45 km (28 miles) northwest of the city centre (for most intercontinental traffic), and **Linate,** about 10 km (6 miles) to the east (mainly for domestic and European flights). There is an STAM coach service between Milan's Stazione Centrale and Linate every 20 minutes. The A.T.M. city bus (73) goes to Piazza San Babila, near Via Monte Napoleone, every 10 minutes. Airpullman services operating between Stazione Centrale and Malpensa connect with scheduled flights.

Alitalia reservations: Milan (02) 147 865642; U.K. 071-602-7111; U.S.A. (212) 582 8900

Malpensa and Linate Airport information: tel. (02) 74852200

Bergamo has an airport (for domestic flights) southwest of town at Orio; tel. (035) 326111.

Where's the bus for Milan? **Dove si trova l'autobus per Milano?**

B

BUDGETING FOR YOUR TRIP

In the Italian economy, inflation is very much a stop-start element, with sudden unpredictable de- and re-valuations. Here are some typical prices in *lire* (L).

Airport bus. Linate: STAM service L4,000, A.T.M. service L1,500; Malpensa L13,000.
Baby-sitters. L10,000–15,000 per hour, plus transport, plus agency fee L10,000.
Camping. L12,000 per person per night (children L3,000); car, caravan (trailer or camper) L14,000 per night; tent L10,000 per night; motorcycle free.
Car hire/rental. Booked on arrival in Milan, with unlimited mileage but collision/theft insurance and 19% tax extra): small (VW Polo) L141,000 per day, L705,000 per week; medium-range (Fiat Tipo) L203,000 per day, L1,015,000 per week.
Entertainment. Cinema L12,000; disco (entrance and first drink) L20,000–40,000; opera L25,000–200,000.
Hotels. Double occupancy per night, including service and taxes, no meals: low L100,000–170,000, moderate L170,000–310,000, luxury L310,000–600,000. (See RECOMMENDED HOTELS on page 129.)
Meals and drinks. Continental breakfast L10,000–25,000; lunch or dinner in fairly good restaurant (including service but not wine) L40,000–80,000; bottle of wine, from L6,000; beer/soft drinks L3,000–8,000; apéritif L3,000–5,000; coffee served at the table L3,500–8,000, at the bar L1,200–1,700.
Museums. L2,000–12,000 (see also page 47).
Public transport. Metro/bus/tram tickets L1,500; day-travel pass L5,000, two-day pass L9,00, one-week pass L20,000.
Shopping bag. 500g bread L1,500, 250g butter L3,000, 500g beefsteak L15,000–20,000, 200g coffee L4,000, bottle of wine L4,000+.

Taxis. From Linate airport L25,000–30,000; from Malpensa airport L150,000; average trip inside Milan L10,000–15,000.
Youth hostels. L24,000 per night, with breakfast.

C

CAMPING *(campeggio)*

You'll find plenty of campsites around the lakes and in the Milan area, notably the one at **Città di Milano,** Via Gaetano Airaghi (near Tangenziale Ovest motorway), tel. (02) 48200134, which is open all year round. Alternatively, another Milan site is out at the **Autodromo di Monza;** tel. (039) 387771. For others, consult the *Yellow Pages* in the telephone directory under *Campeggi-Ostelli-Villaggi Turistici* (Campsites, Hostels, Tourist Villages).

Addresses and details of amenities for the Lombardy region are given in the directory *Campeggi in Italia*, published by the Italian Touring Club (TCI), Corso Italia 10, 20122 Milan, tel. (02) 85261. TCI also operates a bookshop (and travel agency) at the same address that offers books in Italian and English which cover camping and other tourist activities, as well as restaurants and hotels. A free list of sites with a map is available from the Italian National Tourist Office (see page 126).

Campsites at the lakes in July and August are invariably very crowded. Check with local tourist offices (see page 126) about reservations. Many campsites require the *International Camping Carnet*, a pass that entitles holders to modest discounts and insurance coverage throughout Europe. It can be obtained through your camping or automobile association or the TCI.

Is there a campsite near here? **C'è un campeggio qui vicino?**

CAR HIRE/RENTAL *(autonoleggio)*

(See also Driving and Planning Your Budget)

Driving in Milan is not recommended, so in order to save money and allow yourself for more relaxed stay, try to do all your sightseeing in the city first, and then afterward hire a car to take on out-of-town excursions.

For the best deal, reserve your car back home. This can be done either through your travel agent as a package with your flight and hotel booking or directly through a major international car rental company. Check whether the deal includes unlimited mileage, what kind of insurance is available, and if the car has to be returned to its starting point. Some companies charge extra if, for instance, you pick up the car downtown and drop it off at the airport (which may nonetheless be the most desirable arrangement, since you may not need the car until you start your excursions).

To rent a car locally, consult the telephone directory's yellow pages under Autonoleggio and then be prepared to bargain: weekend rates, unlimited mileage, third-party, or full insurance coverage can all make a difference. Major companies usually have English-speaking staff. You will need a driving licence and passport or national identity card. Minimum age is 21 or 25 depending on the company and the car's engine size—or even 30 if an upmarket car is involved. Also, you must have held a licence for at least one year. Without a credit card, the required cash deposit may be prohibitive.

I'd like to hire a car.	**Vorrei noleggiare una macchina.**
for one day/a week	**per un giorno/una settimana**

CLIMATE and CLOTHING

In the Po valley, summers are very hot and humid, winters cold and foggy. Temperatures are at their most extreme in and directly around Milan itself; the lake regions are generally a couple of degrees cooler. The best time to visit Milan is in spring or autumn—between April and June or in September. As the luxuriant vegetation testifies, winters around the lakes can offer some surprisingly mild days, but can also be as bitingly cold as in northern Europe.

Milan's average daily temperatures (minimum pre-dawn, maximum mid-afternoon) are as follows:

		J	F	M	A	M	J	J	A	S	O	N	D
F°	max	40	46	56	65	74	80	84	82	75	63	51	43
	min	32	35	43	49	57	63	67	66	61	52	43	35
C°	max	5	8	13	18	23	27	29	28	24	17	10	6
	min	0	2	6	10	14	17	19	19	16	11	6	2

Clothing. Outside June, July and August, in the city or out at the lakes, pack a sweater for the evenings. You'll need rainwear in spring and autumn, boots and overcoat in the winter. Good walking shoes are essential all year round. When visiting churches, avoid shorts and the "underwear look."

Milan is more formal, more "northern European" than other Italian cities. Suits, jackets, and ties for men, and smarter dresses and suits for women are common for many restaurants. The Milanese—whose professional footballers wear designer gear—appreciate elegance, even in the casualwear accepted in the majority of establishments.

COMPLAINTS (See also ETIQUETTE)

In hotels, restaurants, and shops, complaints should be made directly to the manager (*direttore*) or proprietor (*proprietario*). The threat of formal declaration to the police should be effective in such cases as overcharging for car repairs (but be aware that carrying out the threat may take up a lot of time). Arguments over taxi fares can usually be settled by referring to the notice affixed by law in each taxi, specifying charges in excess of the meter rate.

CRIME and SAFETY

(See also EMERGENCIES and POLICE)

The watchword is prudence, but not paranoia. Petty theft in Italy is an endless annoyance and tourists are always easy targets for robbery. By taking a few simple precautions, you can reduce the risk of theft. First, make sure you have **insurance** to cover theft or loss of personal effects while abroad. Take **traveller's cheques** and change only a minimum of cash. Keep your record of traveller's cheque (and passport) numbers separate from the cheques.

Leave documents and unneeded valuables in the **hotel safe.** Carry money and credit cards in an inside pocket or a pouch inside your clothes. Bags strapped around your waist are convenient, but they are also obvious targets.

Photocopy your tickets, driving licence, passport, and other vital documents to facilitate reporting a theft and obtaining replacements. Leave one set of photocopies at home and carry another set separately from the originals. Never leave valuables in a **parked car,** not even in the boot (trunk). Leave a car containing luggage only in the care of a parking attendant.

Any loss or theft should be reported at once to the nearest police station—if only for insurance purposes. Your insurance company will need to see a copy of the police report.

I want to report a theft.	**Voglio denunciare un furto.**
My ticket/wallet/passport/ handbag/credit card has been stolen.	**Mi hanno rubato il mio biglietto/portafoglio/ passaporto/la mia borsetta/ carta di credito.**

CUSTOMS *(dogana)* and ENTRY REQUIREMENTS

Visitors from EU countries need only a national identity card to enter Italy. Citizens of most other countries must have a valid passport. Though European and North American residents are not subject to any health requirements, visitors from further afield may require a smallpox vaccination. Check with your travel agent before departure.

Duty free. As Italy is part of the EU, free exchange of non-duty-free goods for personal use is permitted between Italy and the U.K. and the Republic of Ireland. However, duty-free items are still subject to restrictions: check before you go. For residents of non-EU countries, restrictions are as follows: **Australia:** 250 cigarettes **or** 250*g* tobacco; 1*l* alcohol; **Canada:** 200 cigarettes **and** 50 cigars **and** 400*g* tobacco; 1.1*l* spirits **or** wine **or** 8.5*l* beer; **New Zealand:** 200 cigarettes **or** 50 cigars **or** 250*g* tobacco; 4.5*l* wine **or** beer **and**

1.1*l* spirits; **South Africa:** 400 cigarettes **and** 50 cigars **and** 250*g* tobacco;2*l* wine **and** 1*l* spirits; **U.S.A.:** 200 cigarettes **and** 100 cigars or 2*kg* of tobacco.

Currency restrictions. Non-residents may import or export up to L200,000 in local currency. There is no limit on the foreign currency or traveller's cheques you may import or export, though amounts in excess of L5,000,000 should be declared at the point of entry.

I've nothing to declare.	**Non ho nullo da dichiarare.**
It's for my personal use.	**È per mio uso personale.**

DRIVING in MILAN (See also CAR HIRE)

To take a car into Italy, you must have:

- a valid national driving licence, International Driving Permit or pink European Union (European Community) licence. It is advisable to carry a translation (free from automobile associations).
- car registration papers.
- Green Card (*carta verde*)—an extension to a regular insurance policy making it valid specifically for Italy; if you plan to stay in Italy for more than 45 days, you must take out Italian insurance.
- red warning triangle—placed at least 30 metres (100 feet) behind the car in emergency.
- national identity sticker for both cars and caravans (trailers).

You must be at least 18 years old to drive a car in Italy. Drivers of motorcycles (any two-wheeler over 49cc) need the same documents as car drivers. Drivers entering Italy in a car not their own must have the owner's written permission.

Fuel and oil (*benzina; olio*). Prices are set by the government. Petrol (gasoline) is available in super (98-100 octane), unleaded (95 octane), normal (86-88 octane) and diesel. Visitors from America should remember that 40 litres is a fraction more than 10 US gallons (see conversion charts on page opposite). Filling stations—most have a self-service pump—generally provide full service 7am to 1:30pm,

3:30 to 7:30pm in summer, closing half an hour earlier in winter. Many close on Sunday. Stations along the *autostrada* open 24 hours a day.

Fluid measures

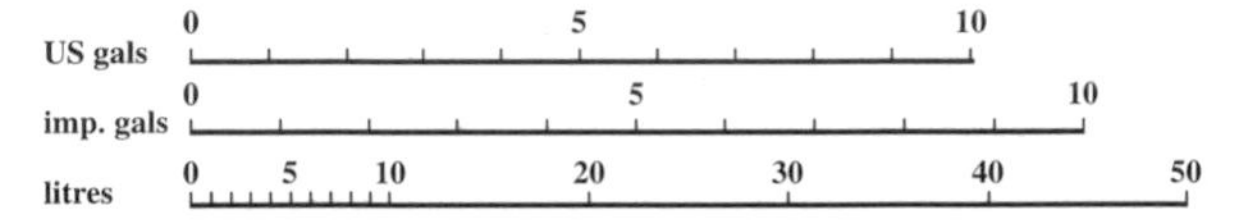

Distance

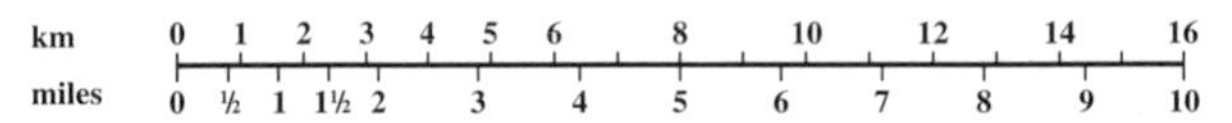

Speed limits on the *autostrada* toll highways are 130 km/h (80 mph) Monday–Friday, 110 km/h (70 mph) Saturday–Sunday and holidays. On other roads the limit is 90 km/h (55 mph), apart from in built-up areas, where it is 50 km/h (30 mph). Speeding fines are high. Pay on the spot; if you don't, the charge is much higher later and the computer will track you down.

Driving conditions. Drive on the right, pass on the left. When overtaking or remaining in the left-hand lane, keep your indicator flashing. Traffic on major roads has right of way over that entering from side roads. At the intersection of roads of similar importance, the car on the right has priority, but take nothing for granted.

In Milan, forget the car. Despite the Italians' instinctive tendency to ignore all restrictions, the ban on private cars in the city centre is taking hold. Computerized parking fines are fast enough to be added on to your car rental credit card bill or to pursue you back home.

Milan drivers pride themselves on being more disciplined than most Italians, but that remains a relative judgement. If you must drive in the city, be firm but not reckless. In a traffic jam, advance steadily and confidently forward. You may cause trouble and win no gratitude by courteously waving on another driver to cut in ahead of you. Most Milanese have Monza-fast reflexes for whipping in and out of available spaces—without your help.

Road conditions. For travel outside Milan, the ACI (*Automobile Club d'Italia*) operates a Rome-based, 24-hour telephone assistance centre staffed with multilingual personnel who give nationwide information on road and weather conditions; tel. (06) 4477. For service in Milan, the ACI office is at Corso Venezia 43; tel. (02) 77451.

Apart from the *autostrada* (motorway/expressway), the road network comprises: *strada statale* (state road), *strada provinciale* (provincial road), and *strada comunale* (local road). Access signs to the *autostrada* are green. Toll charges are regulated according to vehicle size and distance travelled, controlled by a ticket, and paid at the exit, or as a flat rate when joining the motorway.

Accidents and breakdowns. The emergency number is **113,** with telephones at regular intervals on the *autostrada*. The ACI assistance number is **116,** but their service is not free, so take out international breakdown insurance before leaving home.

Parking. Parking in Milan is highly restricted. In areas open to non-residents, a Sostamilano Card, available from authorized retailers and uniformed A.T.M. (*Azienda Transporti Municipali*) personnel, is required to be displayed on the dashboard or rearview mirror. Parking outside the city is highly recommended whenever possible. The A.T.M. operates free parking lots outside the city and the city centre is easily reached by public transport.

Road signs. Most road signs in Italy are international pictographs, but here are some written ones which you may also see:

Accendere le luci	Use headlights
Deviazione	Diversion (Detour)
Divieto di sorpasso	No overtaking (passing)
Divieto di sosta	No stopping
Lavori in corso	Road works (Men working)
Passaggio a livello	Level railway crossing
Pericolo	Danger

Rallentare	Slow down
Senso unico	One-way street
Senso vietato/Vietato l'ingresso	No entry
Uscita	Exit
Zona pedonale	Pedestrian zone
driving licence	**patente**
car registration papers	**libretto di circulazione**
Fill the tank, please.	**Per favore, faccia il pieno.**
Super/normal	**super/normale**
unleaded/diesel	**senza piombo/gasolio**
I've broken down.	**Ho avuto un guasto.**
There's been an accident.	**C'è stato un incidente.**

E

ELECTRICITY

Generally 220 volts, 50 Hz AC, but sometimes 125-volt outlets, with different plugs and sockets for each. If in doubt, ask. An adapter (*presa multipla*) or voltage transformer (*trasformatore*) can be found in Italy, but your best bet is to bring one from home.

EMBASSIES and CONSULATES *(consulato)*

Embassies and consulates are located in either Milan or Rome.

Australia: *Consulate*: Via Borgognone 2, Milan; tel. (02) 777041.

Britain: *Consulate*: Via San Paolo 7, Milan; tel. (02) 723001.

Canada: *Consulate*: Via Vittor Pisani 19, Milan; tel. (02) 67581.

Republic of Ireland: *Embassy*: Largo del Nazareno 3, Rome; tel. (06) 6979121.

New Zealand: *Embassy*: Via Zara 28, Rome; tel. (06) 4402928.

South Africa: *Consulate*: Via San Giovanni sul Muro 4, Milan; tel. (02) 80903069.

U.S.A.: *Consulate*: Via Principe Amedeo 2, Milan; tel. (02) 290351.

EMERGENCIES (See also POLICE and MEDICAL CARE)

The following numbers operate 24 hours a day. If possible, have an Italian-speaker at hand to give your name and whereabouts:

Police, first-aid, ambulance	**113**
Carabinieri (for urgent problems)	**112**
Fire brigade	**115**
ACI (Automobile Club d'Italia)	**116**
Help!	**Aiuto!**
Can you place an emergency call for me to the ...	**Può fare per me una telefonata d'emergenza ...?**
police/hospital/ fire brigade	**alla polizia/all'ospedale/ ai pompieri**

ETIQUETTE (See also TIPPING)

Compared with other Italians, the Milanese are cool but polite. Everybody calls each other *Signora* (madam) or *Signore* (sir). More elevated titles such as *dottore*, *professore,* or *commendatore* (something approaching "milord") are bandied about, regardless of your qualifications, with an Italian blend of good humour and courtesy.

For your part, there a few simple words which should make your stay easier. Preface a request with an Italian variation on "please"—*per piacere, per cortesìa,* or *per favore*—it will at least attract attention. End with a "thank you," *molto grazie* or *grazie tanto*, and when they thank you, remember a little "don't mention it"—*prego*. When entering a shop, don't launch into your inquiry without first saying *buon giorno* (good day) or *buona sera* (good evening); and when making your way through a crowded museum or train, *permesso* (excuse me) will not go unnoticed.

G

GAY and LESBIAN TRAVELLERS

Milan's office for gay men and women is **Arci Gay,** Centro d'Iniziativa Gay, Via Torcello 19; tel./fax (02) 58100399. A monthly magazine, *Babilonia*, provides information about entertainment and services.

GETTING THERE

By Air

Scheduled flights. Most transatlantic flights direct to Milan come into Malpensa, with European and domestic flights arriving at Linate (see AIRPORTS on page 104). These days, the major airlines' special deals like Super APEX are fiercely competitive in price, but be careful about the precise conditions of booking and travel. If you are going elsewhere in Italy, check whether you can fly into Milan and then out from, say, Rome.

Chartered flights and package tours are proposed as all-inclusive arrangements (air fare, accommodation, sightseeing, and airport transfers, combining Milan with one of the lakes) or on an individual basis, tailor-made to your personal requirements with an independent itinerary. Check with local travel agents or at the Compagnia Italian Turismo (CIT), Italy's national travel agency and tour operator. If you're flying by charter with an independent itinerary in mind, ask about fly-drive possibilities combining air fare and car rental. The Italian National Tourist Office (see page 126) has lists of recognized tour operators.

By Road

The Chunnel and car ferries link Britain with France, Belgium, and Holland. Once on the continent, you can put your car on a train to Milan (starting points include Bologne, Paris, and Cologne), or you can drive all the way to Milan without leaving the motorway.

By Rail

Tickets such as **Inter-Rail, Rail Europ Senior** and **Eurailpass** (for non-European residents signing up before leaving home) are valid for travel in Italy, but check on term s and conditions before leaving home. For up-to-date details, consult a travel agency or the Italian National Tourist Office (see page 126). Within Italy, you can obtain an

Italian Tourist Ticket (*Biglietto Turistico di Libera Circolazione*); further details in Milan from Stazione Centrale; tel. (02) 147888088.

GUIDES and TOURS

Many of Milan's larger hotels can arrange for multi-lingual guides or interpreters to accompany either groups or individuals. Tours include both the city of Milan and day-trips to Certoso di Pavia, Bergamo, and lakes Maggiore and Como. Agree on the fee before setting out. A tour-guide service operates from the city tourist office (see page 126), APT, Via Marconi 1 (Metro: Duomo); tel. and fax (02) 725241. A 3-hour bus tour from the tourist office with *Agenzia Auostradale* departs from the Piazzetta Reale alongside the Duomo (departs daily at 9:30am).

We'd like an English-speaking guide.	**Desideriamo una guida che parla inglese.**

H

HEALTH and MEDICAL CARE

(See also EMERGENCIES)

If your health insurance does not cover foreign countries, take out a short-term policy covering illness or accident while you are on holiday. Visitors from European Union countries are entitled to the same health cover as the Italians, but must have a special form from the governmental health authorities.

If you need medical care, your hotel receptionist will help you find an English-speaking doctor (or dentist). Milan's *Servizio di Pronto Soccorso* (First Aid Service) functions day and night at the Policlinico hospital, Via Francesco Sforza 33 (Metro: Crocetta); tel. (02) 55031.

Chemists/Pharmacies. The *farmacia* is open during shopping hours (see OPENING HOURS), and an all-night service is also available at Stazione Centrale (tel. 02-6690735). For information on other pharmacies open after-hours and on Sunday, call (06) 624471. The opening schedule for other duty pharmacies is posted on every pharmacy door and in local newspapers. Bring along an adequate supply of any prescribed medication.

I need a doctor/dentist.	**Ho bisogno di un medico/dentista.**
Where's the nearest (all-night) pharmacy?	**Dov'è la farmacia (di turno) più vicina?**

HOLIDAYS *(festa)*

When a national holiday falls on a Thursday or a Tuesday, Italians may make a *ponte* (bridge) to the weekend, taking Friday or Monday off as well. Banks, government offices, most shops, museums and galleries are closed on the following days:

1 January	*Capodanno/ Primo dell'Anno*	New Year's Day
6 January	*Epifania*	Epiphany
25 April	*Festa della Liberazione*	Liberation Day
1 May	*Festa del Lavoro*	Labour Day
15 August	*Ferragosto*	Assumption Day
1 November	*Ognissanti*	All Saints' Day
7 December	*Sant'Ambrogio*	Milan's Patron Saint Ambrose
8 December	*L'Immacolata Concezione*	Immaculate Conception
25 December	*Natale*	Christmas Day
26 December	*Santo Stefano*	St. Stephen's Day
Movable date	*Lunedì di Pasqua*	Easter Monday

L

LANGUAGE

Staff at the major hotels and shops of Milan and the resorts usually speak some English. Most Italians appreciate foreigners trying to communicate in their language, even if it's only a few words.

DAYS OF THE WEEK

Sunday	**domenica**	Thursday	**giovedì**
Monday	**lunedì**	Friday	**venerdì**
Tuesday	**martedì**	Saturday	**sabato**
Wednesday	**mercoledì**		

MONTHS OF THE YEAR

January	**gennaio**	July	**luglio**
February	**febbraio**	August	**agosto**
March	**marzo**	September	**settembre**
April	**aprile**	October	**ottobre**
May	**maggio**	November	**novembre**
June	**giugno**	December	**dicembre**

NUMBERS

0	**zero**	11	**undici**	30	**trenta**
1	**une**	12	**dodici**	40	**quaranta**
2	**due**	13	**tredici**	50	**cinquanta**
3	**tre**	14	**quattordici**	60	**sessanta**
4	**quattro**	15	**quindici**	70	**settanta**
5	**cinque**	16	**sedici**	80	**ottanta**
6	**sei**	17	**diciassette**	90	**novanta**
7	**sette**	18	**diciotto**	100	**cento**
8	**otto**	19	**diciannove**	101	**centuno**
9	**nove**	20	**venti**	110	**centodieci**
10	**dieci**	21	**ventuno**	1,000	**mille**

LOST PROPERTY

Cynics say anything lost in Italy is lost forever, but that's not necessarily true in Milan. Restaurants more often than not will have your forgotten briefcase, guidebook, or even camera waiting for you at the cashier's desk. If you've lost something away from your hotel, have the receptionist call the town hall's lost property office (*Ufficio Oggetti Smarriti*), Via Friuli 30 (Metro: Duomo); tel. (02) 5465299.

I've lost my handbag/passport/wallet. — **Ho perso la mia borsetta/il mio passaporto/il mio portafoglio.**

MEDIA

Radio and TV (*rádio; televisione*). During the tourist season, RAI, the Italian state radio and TV network, occasionally broadcasts news in English. British (BBC), American (VOA), and Canadian (CBC) programmes are easily obtained on short-wave transistors. RAI television and private channels broadcast exclusively in Italian.

Newspapers and magazines (*giornale; rivista*). Unlike the *International Herald Tribune*, which has an edition printed in Rome, British newspapers may arrive in Milan one day late. Kiosks around the Piazza del Duomo and in major hotels are the best place to find the newsweeklies and other magazines.

For what's on in Milan each week, get *Viva Milano* (published Wednesday) or *Tutto Milano* (Thursday). The main Milan daily is the *Corriere della Sera*, which is venerable in its news coverage and reliable for local entertainment listings (the Wednesday edition has a special section with a list of events). More sprightly is the Rome-based *La Repubblica*, with a large section devoted to life in Milan. This sports-mad country also has a daily paper, *La Gazetta dello Sport*, devoted to events not only in Italy but all over the world.

Have you any English-language newspapers? — **Avete giornali in inglese?**

MONEY

Currency. The *lira* (plural *lire*, abbreviated *L* or *Lit*) is the Italian monetary unit. (For currency restrictions, see CUSTOMS AND ENTRY FORMALITIES.)

Coins: L5, 10, 20, 50, 100, 200, 500.
Banknotes: L1,000, 2,000, 5,000 10,000, 50,000, 100,000.

Exchange facilities. Carry your passport for all exchange transactions. The advantage of the banks' better exchange rate should be weighed against the frequently tiresome wait at their counters. The bank rate will be better than in restaurants or shops. Banks open 8:30am to 1:30pm, some of them reopening 2:30 to 4:30pm. The exchange counters at Linate airport open 8am to 9pm (Malpensa 8pm).

Automatic cash dispensers are the most convenient option, but generally carry a hefty commission. They can be found at the airports, the Stazione Centrale, banks, and the APT tourist information office on the corner of Via Marconi and Piazza del Duomo (see page 126).

Credit cards. Shops, banks, hotels, and an increasing number of restaurants accept major credit cards. The frequently posted *Carta Si* sign means that a wide range of cards are accepted.

Traveller's cheques and Eurocheques are best cashed at the bank or your hotel.

I want to change some pounds/dollars.	**Desidero cambiare delle sterling/dei dollare.**
Do you accept traveller's cheques?	**Accetta traveller's cheques?**
Can I pay with this credit card?	**Posso pagare con la carta di credito?**

O

OPENING HOURS *(orari di apertura)*

(See also PUBLIC HOLIDAYS)

Milan is north European in its habits—less siesta-prone and taking shorter lunch hours than further south.

Banks are generally open Monday–Friday 8:30am–1:30pm, 3–4pm. Currency exchange offices at the airports and railway stations open later and at weekends, too (see MONEY MATTERS).

Churches generally close for sightseeing at lunchtime, noon–3pm.

Museums and **art galleries** constantly change their opening times. Most open 9 or 9:30am with a break for lunch and close on Monday (see also page 47). Check at the tourist information office (see page 126).

Post Offices normally open Monday–Friday 8:05 or 8:30am–2 or 2:30pm (noon Saturday). The main post office at Piazza Cordusio 1 (Metro: Cordusio) provides service weekdays 8:30am–7pm.

Shops in Milan are closed for a half-day Monday morning; food shops for a half day Monday in the afternoon. All are open Tuesday–Saturday 9am–noon, 3:30–7:30pm. Hours are more flexible at the lake resorts.

POLICE (See also CRIME and EMERGENCIES)

The municipal police (*Vigili Urbani*), dressed in navy blue with white helmets or all in white, handle city traffic and other municipal tasks. They are courteous but rarely speak a foreign language –except for a few interpreters wearing a badge.

The *Carabinieri*, who wear black uniforms with a red stripe down the side of the trousers, deal with major crimes and demonstrations. The *Polizia di stato* (national police) man Italy's frontiers, airports, and railway stations.

Emergency number	**113**
Where's the nearest police station?	**Dov'è il più vicino posto di polizia?**

POST OFFICES (*posta or ufficio postale*)

They normally open Monday–Friday 8 or 8:30am to 2 or 2:30pm (noon Saturday). The main post office at Piazza Cordusio 1 (Metro: Cordusio), offers normal mailing facilities and services weekdays from 8:30am until 7pm.

Postage stamps can also be purchased from tobacconists and some hotels. Letter boxes are painted red.

PUBLIC TRANSPORTATION

Buses/trams (*autobus/tram*). The network of bus and tram lines needs a little studying and is perhaps most useful only for longer stays. A map is available from the tourist information office (see page 126), other details from the A.T.M. (*Azienda Trasporti Milanesi*) information office above the Duomo Metro station.

Trains. The Italian State Railway (*Ferrovie dello Stato*) offers a service with fares among the lowest in Europe. The green M2 Metro line serves all of Milan's railway stations to the surrounding region. Journey times vary a good deal, depending on the type of train:

Regionali	Regional intercity express stopping at main regional cities.
Interregionali	Long-distance express stopping at major cities only; first and second class.
EuroCity (EC)	International express; first and second class.
InterCity (IC)	Intercity express with few stops; luxury service with first and second class.
Espresso (EXP)	Long-distance train, stopping at main stations.
Diretto (D)	Slower than *Espresso;* makes a few local stops.
Locale (L)	Local train stopping at almost every station.

Tickets (see also TRAVELLING TO MILAN) can be purchased and reservations made at a local travel agency or at the railway station. Better-class trains have dining cars or self-service cars which offer food and beverages at reasonable prices. If you don't have a reservation, arrive at the station at least 20 minutes before departure; Italy's trains are often crowded.

Taxis. Your best chance of finding one is either at the railway station ranks or near the major hotels. Taxis are relatively cheap by North European and American standards, *if* the meter is running. Extra charges for luggage and night, public holiday, or airport trips should be posted in four languages inside all taxis. A tip of at least 10 percent is customary. Beware of non-metered, unlicensed taxis, whose rates are just like their eloquent Italian name—*abusivi*. Radio-Taxi in Milan: tel. (02) 5251, (02) 6767, (02) 8388, or (02) 8585.

Underground/Subway (*Metrò*). Milan has three underground railway lines coded red (M1), green (M2) and yellow (M3), serving all the major tourist sights. Red and yellow intersect in the city centre at the Duomo. Green and yellow intersect at the Stazione Centrale. A bright red "M" sign marks the station entrances. Tickets are available at newsstands, tobacconists, and Metro stations, and trains run roughly from 6am to just after midnight.

Ferries/Lake Cruises. Tickets for lake cruises can be bought in Milan at: Navigazione Lagho Maggiore, Garda e di Como, Via Lodovico Ariosto 21 (Metro Conciliazione); tel. (02) 4812086, fax (02) 4980628.

Lake Como. For timetables and details about lake cruises contact the head office of Navigazione Lago di Como, Via per Cernobbio 18; tel. (031) 579211. The main towns served by boat and hydrofoil are Como, Tremezzo, Bellagio, Menaggio, and (on west shore) Varenna and Lecco. A car ferry links Bellagio, Cadenabbia, Varenna, and Menaggio.

Lake Garda. You can cruise from Desenzano all the way north to Riva del Garda in just over four hours. The pride of the fleet is a paddle steamer built in 1901, but there are also more modern motor boats, hydrofoils, and car ferries. An attractive feature is the summer season ticket, which lets you cruise as often as you like anywhere on the lake within a specific period. Timetable and ticket details are available from Navigazione Lago di Garda, Piazza Matteotti 2, Desenzano sul Garda; tel. (030) 9149511.

Lake Maggiore. To see Lake Maggiore from the water, take a cruise anywhere between Arona at the southern end and Cannobio in the north, or even over the Swiss border all the way to Locarno. For timetables and other details in advance, contact Navigazione Lago Maggiore, Viale F Baracca 1, Arona; tel. (0322) 233200, fax (0332) 249530. Tickets can be bought at any of the stops on the way, which include Stresa, Baveno, Pallanza, Verbania, and Laveno. The company has a fleet of 30 vessels serving the whole lake, either rapid hydrofoils or more leisurely boats with restaurants and bars. A popular favourite is the old fashioned *Piemonte* steamer built in 1904. The most luxurious of the modern boats is the *Verbania*, carrying up to 1,000 passengers with a 360-seat restaurant.

R

RELIGION

Roman Catholic mass is celebrated daily (several times on Sunday) in Italian. Information about Protestant services may be obtained from Ciese Christiane Protestanti, at Marchi 9; tel. (02) 6552858; and Via P.L. Palestrina 14, tel. (02) 66987408.

Jewish Sabbath and holy days are celebrated by the *Comunità Ebraica di Milano* (Milan Hebrew Community), Via Papa Leone XIII, tel. (02) 4815806 (behind Parco Sempione); tel. (02) 4815806; and Via S. Mayer 4/6, tel. (02) 4152149.

For Moslems, the *Istituto Culturale Islamica* is at Viale Edoardo Jenner 50; tel. (02) 6071856.

T

TELEPHONES *(telefono)*

Besides public telephone booths in the streets, you can call from almost every bar or café (usually displaying a yellow telephone sign), where you pay at the counter after the call. Some older types of public phones require tokens (*gettoni*) with a value of 200 lire (available at bars, post offices and tobacconists).

Magnetic phone cards with a value of 6,000 or 9,000 lire are issued from offices of the SIP (Italian Telephone Service). For direct dialling abroad, use telephones labelled *Teleselezione.* To make an international call, dial 00 and wait for a change of tone before dialling the country code of the country you want to reach, area code and subscriber's number.

The country code for Italy is **39.** When dialing from outside the country you do not need to dial the **0** at the beginning off the city or area code, which is included in all the numbers listed in this book. The "0" must be dialed as part of the city code when calling from another city within Italy. Note that local numbers in Italy range from four to eight digits.

Fax is available at the main Cordusio post office (see above) and at the Stazione Centrale office, open Monday–Friday 8:15am–7:30pm (3:30pm Saturday), closed Sunday.

Local directory and other Italian enquiries	**12**
European international operator	**15**
Intercontinental operator	**170**

Can you get me this number in ...? — **Può passarmi questo numero a ...?**

TIME DIFFERENCES

Italy follows Central European Time and from late March to September clocks are put one hour ahead. The following chart shows times across the world in summer.

New York	London	**Milan**	Jo'burg	Sydney	Auckland
6am	11am	**noon**	noon	8pm	10pm

TIPPING

A service charge is added to most restaurant bills, but it is customary to leave an additional tip. It is also in order to tip bellboys, doormen, hat-check attendants, garage attendants, etc.

Hotel porter, per bag	L2,000
Hotel maid, per day	L2,000
Lavatory attendant	L500–1,000
Waiter	5–10%

Taxi driver	10–15%
Tour guide	10–15%

TOURIST INFORMATION OFFICES

The Italian National Tourist Office (ENIT, *Ente Nazionale Italiano per il Turismo*) publishes detailed brochures with up-to-date information on Milan, Lombardy, and the lakes. They cover transport and accommodation (including campsites), and make suggestions for specialized itineraries. The Italian National Tourist Office can be found abroad in the following locations:

Australia and New Zealand: c/o Italian Government Tourist Office, Minato Ku, Tokyo 107, Japan; tel. (03) 3478-2051.

Canada: 1 Place Ville-Marie, Suite 1914, Montreal, Quebec H3B 3M9; tel. (514) 866-7669, fax (514) 392-1429.

Republic of Ireland: E.N.I.T. London, 1 Princes Street, London W1R 8AY; tel. (171) 408-1254; fax (171) 493-6695.

U.K.: 1 Princes Street, London W1R 8AY; tel. (171) 408-1254,fax (171) 493-6695.

U.S.A.: Chicago: 401 N. Michigan Avenue, Suite 1046, Chicago, Illinois 60611; tel. (312) 644-0990, fax (312) 644-3019. Los Angeles: 12400 Wilshire Boulevard, Suite 550, Los Angeles, CA 90025; tel. (310) 820-0098, fax (310) 820-6357. New York: 630 Fifth Avenue, Suite 1565, New York, NY 10011; tel. (212) 245-4822/5618, fax (212) 586-9249.

Locally, you will find municipal or regional offices (*APT, Azienda di promozione turistica*) in Milan and all the major resort towns. These can be particularly helpful with information (but not reservations) for last-minute accommodation needs.

Bergamo: A.P.T.; Via Vittorio Emanuele 20; 24100 Bergamo; tel. (035) 213185; fax (035) 230184.

Brescia: Corso Zanardelli 38, 25121 Brescia; tel. (030) 45052 or (030) 43418, fax (030) 293284.

Como: Piazza Cavour 17; tel. (031) 3300111, fax (031) 261152.

Milan: Via Marconi 1, 20123 Milan (Metro: Duomo); tel. (02) 725241, fax (02) 72524250 (Secretariat) or (02) 72022999 (Information Office); Stazione Centrale: Galleria di Testa; tel. (02) 6690432 or (02) 6690532.

Monza: Piazza Communale; tel./fax (039) 323222.

Pavia: Via F Filzi 2; tel. (0382) 22156, fax (0382) 32221.

Stresa: Via Prinipe Tomaso 70; tel. (0323) 30150, fax (0323) 32561.

Varese: Via Carrobbio 1; tel. (0332) 283604.

TRAVELLERS WITH DISABILITIES

Italy is not at the forefront of catering to the needs of tourists who are disabled, hard of hearing or blind. Public transport is not yet equipped to lift wheelchairs onto buses or trains, but hotels increasingly do provide appropriate facilities. Lists of such hotels are available from the Italian national tourist office (see page 126) and CIT Italian travel agency in your home country. Museums are also beginning to install elevators for access to exhibition halls on upper floors.

Associazione Italiana Diabili, Via Santa Barnaba 29; tel. (02) 55017564, gives information and advice to travellers with disabilities.

WEIGHTS and MEASURES (See also DRIVING)

Length

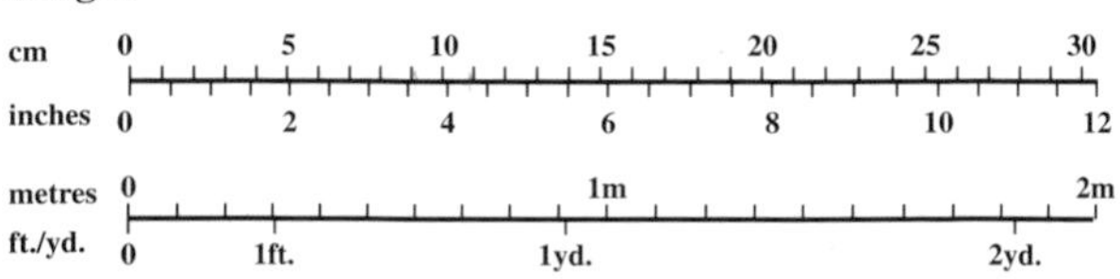

Weight

grams	0	100	200	300	400	500	600	700	800	900	1kg

ounces	0	4	8	12	1lb	20	24	28	2lb

Temperature

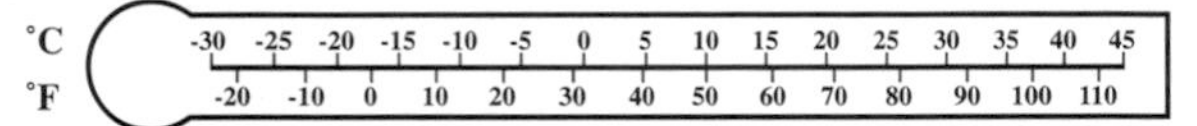

WOMEN TRAVELLERS

Women travelling alone will be bothered much less by Italian males in Milan and Lombardy than those further south. The region prides itself on its more "dignified northern European" attitudes. Indeed, Milanese show a more businesslike, pragmatic approach to life than many of their fellow countrymen. In case of trouble, one phrase worth knowing is:

Lasciatemi in pace! Leave me alone!

YOUTH HOSTELS *(ostello della Gioventù)*

(See also MONEY MATTERS)

If you do not already have an international youth hostel card (*carta IYHF*; no age limit/restrictions), you can obtain one from the Milan office of the Touring Club Italiano, Corso Italia 10 (Metro Missori); tel. (02) 85261, which also issues a hostel guide. Alternatively, cards can also be bought directly from the Milan hostel west of the city centre, near San Siro racecourse:

AIG Ostello Rotta, Via Salonairaghi 2; tel./fax (02) 39267095, 5–11:30pm. Take number 1 Metro Red Line to QT8.

Recommended Hotels

Our selection of hotels concentrates principally on Milan and the resort towns on Lakes Maggiore, Como, and Garda, with a few suggestions for other towns mentioned in our excursions, Monza, Pavia, and Bergamo and—as convenient stopovers to and from the lakes—Varese and Brescia. Prices vary according to season, fluctuations in exchange rates, and Italy's unpredictable inflation.

At last inspection, our hotels all met international standards of cleanliness and comfort. All except some cheaper establishments have rooms with bath and accept the major credit cards. Unless otherwise stated, they are open year round. As the country's business capital, Milan is more expensive than other Italian destinations, but the quality of service is correspondingly good. Except for the top range of the major lake resort towns, prices are lower away from Milan. For our price-range categories, we have used the following symbols (double occupancy, including service and taxes, but with meals extra):

❁	below 120,000 lire
❁❁	120,000–250,000 lire
❁❁❁	above 250,000 lire

MILAN

Ambrosiano ❁❁ *Via Santa Sofia 9; Tel. (02) 58306044, fax (02) 58305067.* Modern hotel, handy for city centre and Navigli district. Closed August and Christmas. 79 rooms.

Arno ❁ *Via Lazzaretto 17; Tel. (02) 6705509.* Family-style hotel conveniently located near the station.

Arthur ❁ *Via Lazzaretto 14; Tel. (02) 2046294.* Clean, plain comfort near the station; showers separate.

Bonaparte ❁❁❁ *Via Cusani 13; Tel. (02) 8560, fax (02) 8693601.* Tasteful, luxurious hotel situated in the heart of the business quarter. 65 rooms.

Capitol ❁❁❁ *Via Cimaroso 6; Tel. (02) 48003050, fax (02) 4694724.* Trade-fair location, and handy for chic boutiques, too. Friendly service. Closed August. 96 rooms.

Carrobbio ❁❁❁ *Via Medici 3; Tel. (02) 89010740, fax (02) 8053334.* A short distance to the Duomo; stylish décor. Closed August and Christmas. 35 rooms.

Cavour ❁❁ *Via Fatebenefratelli 21; Tel. (02) 6572051, fax (02) 6592263.* A no-nonsense downtown hotel close to La Scala. 113 rooms.

De la Ville ❁❁❁ *Via Hoepli 6; Tel. (02) 867651, fax (02) 866609.* Great for the Duomo, opera, and shopping. Elegant interiors and bar. 109 rooms.

Duca di Milano ❁❁❁ *Piazza della Repubblica 13; Tel. (02) 6284, fax (02) 6555966.* The ultimate in luxury business hotels, but with intimate design. 99 suites.

Excelsior Gallia ❁❁❁ *Piazza Duca d'Aosta 9; Tel. (02) 6785, fax (02) 66713239.* Situated near the main station, this is a grand institution offering old-fashioned comfort. 252 rooms.

Four Seasons ❁❁❁ *Via Gesù 8; Tel. (02) 77088, fax (02) 77085000.* Luxury five-star hotel with superb service and ambience. 98 rooms.

Grand Hotel Brun ❁❁❁ *Via Caldera 21; Tel. (02) 45271, fax (02) 48204746.* Convenient for any trade fair (and the football stadium); a great piano bar. 330 rooms.

Grand Hotel Duomo ❁❁❁ *Via San Raffaele 1; Tel. (02) 8833, fax (02) 86462027.* A monument in its own right, on the cathedral square; spectacular roof-terrace. 160 rooms.

London ❁ *Via Rovello 3; Tel. (02) 72020166, fax (02) 8057037.* Central, simple, and clean; warm service; showers separate. Closed August and Christmas. 29 rooms.

Manin ❁❁❁ *Via Manin 7; Tel. (02) 6596511, fax (02) 6552160.* Friendly, family-run hotel overlooking the public gardens. Closed 7–30 August. 118 rooms.

Michelangelo ❁❁❁ *Via Scarlatti 33; Tel. (02) 6755, fax (02) 6694232.* Next to main station; functional comfort. 300 rooms.

Palace ❁❁❁ *Piazza della Repubblica 20; Tel. (02) 6336, fax (02) 654485.* The best of imperial Napoleonic luxury; houses one of Milan's best restaurants, the Casanova Grill (see page 138). 216 rooms.

Pensione Argentario ❁ *Corsa Porta Vittoria 58; Tel. (02) 5464532.* Location is quite central; impeccably clean, with friendly service.

Pensione Jolande ❁ *Corso Magenta 78; Tel. (02) 463317, fax (02) 48019012.* Small, quiet, and clean establishment, very handy for Leonardo da Vinci's *Last Supper.* 23 rooms.

Pierre ❁❁❁ *Via Edmondo de Amicis 32; Tel. (02) 72000581 or 8052157.* Witty combination of ultramodern electronics with tasteful design and personal touch. 49 rooms.

Principe di Savoia ❁❁❁ *Piazza della Repubblica 17; Tel. (02) 6230, fax (02) 6595838.* Grand, 19th-century-style prestige, but with all the modern comforts. 299 rooms.

Sempione ❁ *Via Finocchiaro Aprile 11; Tel. (02) 6570323, fax (02) 6575379.* A quiet and friendly establishment; centrally located. 45 rooms.

Spadari ❁❁❁ *Via Spadari 11; Tel. (02) 72002371, fax (02) 861184.* Charming modern design; refined attention to detail; close to cathedral. Closed 3 days in August and at Christmas. 39 rooms.

Starhotel Ritz ❁❁❁ *Via Spallanzani 40; Tel. (02) 2055, fax (02) 29518679.* Modern, efficient business hotel, near the Duomo and shopping district. 207 rooms.

Valley ❁ *Via Soperga 19; Tel. (02) 6692777, fax (02) 66987252.* Modern, quiet, and clean establishment near the railway station. 12 rooms.

BERGAMO

Agnello d'Oro ❁❁ *Via Gombito 22 (Città Alta); Tel. (035) 249883, fax (035) 235612.* Exquisite little restaurant-hotel in Bergamo's historic centre. 12 rooms.

Il Gourmet ❁❁ *Via San Vigilio 1; Tel. and fax (035) 256110.* Charming old inn with a garden in Città Alta. 11 rooms.

San Georgio ❁ *Via San Giorgio 10; Tel. (035) 212043, fax (035) 310072.* Clean, friendly service, not far from station. 37 rooms.

BRESCIA

Ca'Noa ❀❀ *Via Triumplina 66, Brescia; Tel. (030) 398762, fax (030) 398764.* Modern elegance in quiet garden on city outskirts; swimming pool, health club, sauna. 79 rooms.

Vittoria ❀❀❀ *Via 10 Giornate 20, Brescia; Tel. (030) 280061, fax (030) 280065.* Grand Neo-Classical 1930s style in city centre. 65 rooms.

MONZA

De la Ville ❀❀❀ *Viale Regina Margherita 15; Tel. (039) 382581, fax (039) 367647.* Grand Prix racers' choice near the Villa Reale park. Closed August and Christmas. 55 rooms.

PAVIA

Moderno ❀❀ *Viale Vittorio Emanuele 41; Tel. (0382) 303401, fax (0382) 25225.* Unpretentious elegance, close to Pavia's railway station. Closed one week in August and at Christmas. 54 rooms.

VARESE

Palace ❀❀❀ *Via Luciano Manaro 11; Tel. (0332) 312600, fax (0332) 312870.* Old-fashioned luxury in superb hilltop park in easy reach of Lake Maggiore. 108 rooms.

LAKE MAGGIORE

Bristol ❀❀❀ *Corso Umberto 75, Stresa; Tel. (0323) 32601, fax (0323) 33622.* Lakeside hotel. Gardens, luxurious rooms, indoor and outdoor pools, watersports. Closed mid-November through February. 240 rooms.

Gigi ❀ *Piazzetta San Michele 1, Stresa; Tel. (0323) 30225.* Small, quiet hotel near the lake. Closed November through March. 7 rooms.

Grand Hôtel des Iles Borromées ❁❁❁ *Corso Umberto 67, Stresa; Tel. (0323) 30431, fax (0323) 32405.* A monument among resort hotels since 1861, set in a superb lakefront park. Modern comforts; tennis, golf, sauna, and two swimming pools. 182 rooms.

Regina Palace ❁❁❁ *Corso Umberto 27, Stresa; Tel. (0323) 933777, fax (0323) 933776.* Lakefront view of the Borromean Islands, Belle Epoque décor. Tennis, squash, sauna, and swimming pool. Closed November-March. 166 rooms.

Rigoli ❁ *Via Piave 48, Baveno; Tel. (0323) 924756, fax (0323) 925156.* Lakefront view of the Borromean Islands; convenient location for cruises. North of Stresa. 31 rooms.

Verbano ❁❁ *Isola Pescatori, Via Ugo Ara 2, (Borromean Islands); Tel. (0323) 30408, fax (0323) 33129.* Peace and tranquillity on this small island; summer meals on terrace. 12 rooms.

Villaminta ❁❁ *Via Nazionale del Sempione 123, Stresa; Tel. (0323) 933818, fax (0323) 933955.* North of town, with a lakefront view of the Borromean Islands. Flower gardens, tennis, swimming pool, beach. Closed from November through March. 62 rooms.

LAKE COMO

Barchetta Excelsior ❁❁❁ *Piazza Cavour 1, Como; Tel. (031) 3221, fax (031) 302622.* Facing Lake Como and near the cathedral, with good restaurant. 85 rooms.

Belvedere ❁ *Bellágio; Tel. (031) 950410, fax (031) 950102.* View of Lake Como, and private swimming pool. Closed mid-October to April. Northeast of Como. 50 rooms.

Grand Hôtel Villa d'Este ❁❁❁ *Via Regina 40, Cernobbio; Tel. (031) 511471, fax (031) 512027.* Palatial resort-hotel; 16th-century villa in lakefront gardens, with golf, tennis, squash, three swimming pools, watersports. Closed from December to February. 158 rooms.

Il Griso ❁❁ *Via Provinciale 51, Malgrate; Tel. (0341) 202040, fax (0341) 202248.* Charming modern comfort in delightful lakeside setting. Swimming pool, watersports, and gourmet restaurant. South of Lecco. 46 rooms.

Quarcino ❁❁ *Salida Quarcino 4, Como; Tel. (031) 303934, fax (031) 304678.* Simple comfort in the heart of Como's old town. 13 rooms.

Tremezzo Palace ❁❁❁ *Via Regina 8, Tremezzo; Tel. (0344) 40446, fax (0344) 40201.* 19th-century-style lakefront park, with tennis and swimming pool. Closed Christmas. 100 rooms.

Tre Re ❁❁ *Via Boldoni 20, Como; Tel. (031) 265374, fax (031) 241349.* Quiet location near the cathedral. Closed at Christmas. 45 rooms.

Villa Flori ❁❁❁ *Via Cernobbio 12, Como; Tel. (031) 573105, fax (031) 570379.* Situated west of town, with lakefront gardens and mountain backdrop. Closed Christmas. 45 rooms.

LAKE GARDA

All'Azzurro ❁ *Porto Vecchio, Limone; Tel. (0365) 954000.* Small balconied rooms overlooking the lake. 53 rooms. Closed November through March.

Gargnano Albergo Bogliaco ❁ *Via C. Battisti 4, Limone; Tel. (0365) 71404.* A picturesque port-side inn with pleasant garden. Closed November through Easter.

Grand Hotel Fasano ✿✿✿ *Via Zanardelli 160, Fasano, Gardone Riviera; Tel. (0365) 290220, fax (0365) 290221.* An old Habsburg hunting lodge situated in a beautiful lakeside park. Tennis, swimming pool, beach. Closed mid-October through March. 70 rooms.

Le Palme ✿✿ *Porto Vecchio, Limone; Tel. (0365) 954681, fax (0365) 954239.* Cozy, quiet lakeside hotel with a garden. 28 rooms.

Montefiori ✿✿ *Via dei Lauri 8, Gardone Riviera; Tel. (0365) 290235, fax (0365) 21488.* Three small villas situated in a park overlooking lake. Tennis and swimming. Closed November. 40 rooms.

Romantik Hotel Laurin ✿✿✿ *Viale Landi 9, Salò; Tel. (0365) 22022, fax (0365) 22382.* Belle Epoque elegance, with fine garden and modern watersports facilities. Closed Christmas. 35 rooms.

Villa Cortine ✿✿✿ *Via Grotte 6, Sirmione; Tel. (030) 9905890, fax (030) 916390.* Neo-Classical décor in magnificent lakeside gardens. Tennis, swimming pool, private beach. Closed November to March. 55 rooms.

Villa del Sogno ✿✿✿ *Via Zanardelli 107, Fasano, Gardone Riviera; Tel. (0365) 290181, fax (0365) 290230.* Grand lakeside gardens, tennis, sauna, pool. Closed mid-October to March. 35 rooms.

Villa Fiordaliso ✿✿✿ *Via Zanardelli 132, Gardone Riviera; Tel. (0365) 20158, fax (0365) 290011.* Small, luxury Belle Epoque hotel with gourmet restaurant. Closed January through February. 7 rooms.

Villa Rosa ✿ *Via San Quasimodo 4, Sirmione; Tel. (030) 9196320.* Friendly family hotel with garden.

Recommended Restaurants

Our choice ranges from simple trattorias to chic restaurants, occasionally recommending establishments attached to hotels. The Italians are, perhaps understandably, so enamoured of their own cuisine that there is less choice of Oriental or other cuisines and the quality of their own "fast food"—pizzas and toasted sandwiches—reduces the attraction of the hamburger chains. Here, we stick to the Italians.

In Milan, apart from hotel restaurants, most but not all close on Sundays. In the country, closing days vary—so be sure to check when making reservations. (The area code is necessary only when dialling from out of town.) The warning about Milan prices applies as much to restaurants as to hotels. Once again, meals are cheaper away from the metropolis. For our three price-range categories, the following symbols cover a three-course meal, 15% service, but not wine:

❁	below 50,000 lire
❁❁	50,000–80,000 lire
❁❁❁	above 80,000 lire

CENTRAL MILAN

Bagutta ❁❁❁ *Via Bagutta 14; Tel. (02) 76002767, fax (02) 799613.* Perennially fashionable and celebrated rendezvous for Milanese writers and artists. Great pasta and veal scaloppini.

Biffi Scala ❁❁❁ *Piazza della Scala; Tel. (02) 866651, fax (02) 86461070.* Opera's elegant canteen for divas and maestros, famous for their salads and *risotto*.

Peck ❁❁❁ *Via Victor Hugo 4; Tel. (02) 876774, fax (02) 860408.* An appropriate address for the subtle combination of

French and Italian cuisine served at this restaurant. Try any of the following: *ravioli au foie gras*, *osso buco*, and veal kidneys.

NORTH OF CENTRE

Alfredo-Gran San Bernardo ❁❁❁ *Via Borgese 14; Tel. (02) 3319000.* Dignified family service for traditional cuisine: *osso buco* and *cotoletta alla milanese.*

Alla Cucina delle Langhe ❁❁ *Corso Como 6; Tel. (02) 6554279, fax (02) 29006859.* Friendly family bustle and lively atmosphere, as well as splendid *gnocchi* (potato dumplings).

Casanova Grill ❁❁❁ *Piazza della Repubblica 20; Tel. (02) 29000803.* One of the best Milanese restaurants and a favourite with business people; good turbot.

Cuccuma ❁ *Via Pacini 26; Tel. (02) 2663860.* Pleasant Neapolitan trattoria behind main station.

Gianni e Dorina ❁❁ *Via Guglielmo Pepe 38; Tel. (02) 606340.* Friendly service for refined cooking: chestnut ricotta lasagne, quail, and rabbit.

Montecristo ❁❁❁ *Corso Sempione 17; Tel. (02) 312760, fax (02) 3495049.* Seafood for business people, and for lovers, in the candlelit cellar.

Pesa ❁❁ *Viale Pasubio 10; Tel. (02) 6555741.* Family trattoria; traditional Lombard cooking: superb veal, *risotto*.

Riccione ❁❁❁ *Via Taramelli 70; Tel. (02) 683807, fax (02) 66803616.* Elegant seafood restaurant popular with politicians.

SOUTH OF CENTRE

Al Porto ❁❁❁ *Piazzale Generale Cantore; Tel. (02) 8321481, fax (02) 8321481.* Excellent seafood dishes served with charm. The scampi is highly recommended.

Binari ❁❁ *Via Tortona 1; Tel. (02) 89406753.* Classic cuisine served in old-fashioned Milanese décor.

Dongiò ❁ *Via B.Corio 3; Tel. (02) 5511372.* Offers savoury Calabrian cooking, including pasta, *gnocchi,* and good veal dishes.

NAVIGLI (CANAL DISTRICT)

El Brellin ❁❁ *Alzaia Naviglio Grande 14; Tel. (02) 58101351.* Charming terraced trattoria in the Navigli canal district serving traditional local cuisine and old-fashioned recipes.

Montalcino ❁❁ *Via Valenza 17; Tel. (02) 8321926.* Classic Tuscan cuisine. The sophisticated soups, calf's liver, and pasta in wine sauces are excellent.

Posto di Conversazione ❁❁ *Alzaia Naviglio Grande 6; Tel. (02) 58106646.* Inventive cuisine for an old canal-district trattoria: fish, ham, and goose are some of the specialities.

Scaletta ❁❁❁ *Piazzale Stazione Genova 3; Tel. (02) 58100290.* Creative *haute cuisine* near Genova Station; it ranks among the top 15 restaurants in Italy.

BERGAMO

Agnello d'Oro ❁❁❁ *Via Gombito 22, Città Alta; Tel. (035) 249883.* Try any of the following renowned Bergamo dishes: *risotto*, soups, polenta, and pastas at their best, with rabbit, veal, or snails—all served in exquisite décor.

Marianna ❁❁ *Largo Colle Aperto, Città Alta; Tel. (035) 237027.* Marianna's delightful summer terrace is ideal for sampling the classic cuisine: seafood, pasta, and rabbit dishes.

Musicanti ❁❁ *Via San Vigilio, Città Alta; Tel. (035) 253179.* Traditional *gnocchi, risotto,* and seafood pasta dishes are complemented by the restaurant's friendly family atmosphere.

Trattoria del Teatro ❀❀ *Piazza Mascheroni 3; Tel. (035) 238862.* This trattoria, popular with the young crowd, serves up classic cooking.

Vittorio ❀❀❀ *Viale Papa Giovanni XXIII 21, Città Bassa; Tel. (035) 218060.* Considered to be one of Italy's leading restaurants, serving regional specialities in grand style; also duck carpaccio, artichoke soufflé.

MONZA

St. Georges Premier ❀❀❀ *Porta Vedano; Tel. (039) 320600.* Handy for the Grand Prix race track; high-class cuisine served in the setting of an elegant 17th-century villa.

PAVIA

Al Cassinino ❀❀❀ *Via Cassinino 1; Tel. (0382) 422097.* Stylish restaurant, off the road from Certosa, serving varied poultry and seafood menu as well as home-grown vegetables.

Bixio ❀❀ *Tre Re; Tel. (0382) 553588.* Smart seafood restaurant also serving fine rabbit and veal.

Previ ❀❀ *Via Milazzo 65; Tel. (0382) 26203.* Friendly tavern; savoury soups, *risotto*, regional meat dishes.

Vecchio Mulino ❀❀❀ *Via al Monumento 5, Certosa di Pavia; Tel. (0382) 925894.* Refined cuisine (duck, wild game, snails) in an old millhouse décor in Certosa park.

VARESE

Gestore ❀❀ *Piazza Giovine Italia 7, Varese; Tel. (0332) 236404.* Country-style cuisine, with wild game specialities served in season, including hare, pigeon, and pheasant dishes.

Lago Maggiore ❀❀❀ *Via Carrobio 19, Varese; Tel. (0332) 231183.* Creative use of fresh produce: quail and trout dishes, and fine *safran risotto*.

LAKE MAGGIORE

Campanile ❁❁ *Via Montegrappa 16, Baveno; Tel. (0323) 922377.* Classic pasta dishes in charming old house situated north of Stresa.

Cesare ❁❁ *Via Mazzini 14, Stresa; Tel. (0323) 31386.* Set back from the lake; serves classically prepared veal, rabbit, and seafood.

L'Emiliano ❁❁❁ *Corso Italia 50, Stresa; Tel. (0323) 31396.* Stylish setting for imaginative cuisine—lamb, quail, and scampi—in one of Italy's top restaurants.

Piemontese ❁❁ *Via Mazzini 25, Stresa; Tel. (0323) 30235.* Superb seafood pasta and meat dishes; outdoors in summer.

Rigoli ❁❁ *Via Piave 48, Baveno; Tel. (0323) 924756.* Traditional cuisine; quiet location.

Torchio ❁❁ *Via Manzoni, Pallanza; Tel. (0323) 503352.* Cozy, rustic setting for rabbit and pigeon, as well as lake-fish dishes.

Verbano ❁❁ *Isola dei Pescatori (Borromean Islands); Tel. (0323) 30408.* Good classic cuisine in delightful garden facing Isola Bella.

LAKE COMO

Al Giardino ❁❁❁ *Via Montegrappa 52, Como; Tel. (031) 265016.* Fresh lake-fish and seafood in elegant garden villa.

Bilacus ❁❁ *Salita Serbelloni 28, Bellágio; Tel. (031) 950480.* Fresh fish from the lake, well prepared. Northeast of Como.

Bisbino ❁ *Via Statale 31, Mezzegra; Tel. (0344) 40492.* Classic pasta and *risotto* dishes. North of Como.

Brienno ❁❁❁ *Crotto dei Platani, Brienno, Como; Tel. (031) 814038.* Quiet location on Lake Como's west shore. Traditional array of pastas and a wide variety of lake fish are the specialities of the house. Friendly service.

Busciona ❁❁ *Via Valassina, Bellágio; Tel. (031) 964831.* Friendly trattoria in Bellágio, with a fabulous lake view.

Casa di Lucia ❁ *Via Lucia 27, Acquate, Lecco; Tel. (0341) 494594.* Grand 18th-century inn in Lecco, right at the eastern tip of the lake, serving simple country meals, including rabbit, tripe, and pasta.

Cenobio ❁❁ *Via Regina 18, Cernobbio; Tel. (031) 512710.* Classic cuisine in small resort northwest of Como. Summer service in garden.

Il Griso ❁❁❁ *Via Provinciale 51, Malgrate Tel. (0341) 202040* Charming lakeside garden, inventive cuisine: rabbit, fish, and frog's-leg ravioli. South of Lecco. One of Italy's best restaurants.

Porticciolo ❁❁❁ *Via Valsecchi 5, Lecco; Tel. (0341) 498103.* Romantic fireside dinners in winter, summer in the garden. Sophisticated seafood and pasta.

Sant'Anna ❁❁ *Via Turati 1, Como; Tel. (031) 505266.* Cosy refinement for fine veal dishes and fresh lake-fish.

LAKE GARDA

Antica Trattoria delle Rose ❁❁ *Via Gasparo da Salò 33, Salò; Tel. (0365) 43220.* Rustic décor for imaginatively prepared lake-fish specialities; great antipasti.

Campagnola ❁❁ *Via Brunati 11, Salò; Tel. (0365) 22153.* Pleasant family service; fresh vegetables, lake-fish, delicious pasta.

Capriccio ❁❁❁ *Piazza San Bernardo 6, Montinelle, Manerba; Tel. (0365) 551124.* Delightful lakeside terrace for summer service of inventive seafood cuisine; excellent pasta.

Castello Malvezzi ❁❁❁ *Via Colle San Giuseppe 1, Desenzano del Garda; Tel. (030) 2004224.* In a 16th-century castle, fish specialities from nearby Lake Garda, fine pasta and *risotto.*

Cavallino ❁❁❁ *Via Murachette 29, Desenzano del Garda; Tel. (030) 9120217.* Garden and terrace for lake-fish specialities, quail, and pigeon.

Esplanade ❁❁❁ *Via Lario 10, Desenzano del Garda; Tel. (030) 9143361.* Lakeside garden; creative seafood and duck dishes.

Gallo d'Oro ❁❁ *Piazza San Martino 3, Moniga; Tel. (0365) 502405.* Imaginative combinations of seafood and meat dishes.

Gallo Rosso ❁❁❁ *Vicolo Tolacelli 4, Salò; Tel. (0365) 520757.* In comfortable setting, fine seafood, pasta, and *risotto.*

Lorenzaccio ❁❁ *Via Cipro 78, Brescia; Tel. (030) 220457.* Family restaurant, meat dishes.

Piazzetta ❁❁ *Via Indipendenza 87c Sant'Eufemia della Fonte, Desenzano del Garda; Tel. (030) 362668.* Friendly service in stylish atmosphere; imaginative seafood and pasta dishes.

La Sosta ❁❁❁ *Via San Martino della Battaglia 20, Biescia; Tel. (030) 295603.* Set in 17th-century Palazzo Martinengo delle Palle; refined seafood grilled or in *risotto* and pasta.

Tortuga ❁❁❁ *Via 24 Maggio 7, Gargnano; Tel. (0365) 71251,* In elegant setting, creative cuisine with lake-fish and locally grown vegetables.

Villa Fiordaliso ❁❁❁ *Via Zanardelli 132, Gardone Riviera; Tel. (0365) 20158.* Sophisticated cuisine in luxurious lakeside Belle Epoque villa.

ABOUT BERLITZ

In 1878 Professor Maximilian Berlitz had a revolutionary idea about making language learning accessible and enjoyable. One hundred and twenty years later these same principles are still successfully at work.

For language instruction, translation and interpretation services, cross-cultural training, study abroad programs, and an array of publishing products and additional services, visit any one of our more than 350 Berlitz Centers in over 40 countries.

Please consult your local telephone directory for the Berlitz Center nearest you or visit our web site at http://www.berlitz.com.

BERLITZ
Fremdsprachen

Helping the World Communicate